Harvey A. Hornstein

Cruelty and Kindness

a new look at

aggression and altruism

A SPECTRUM BOOK

Prentice-Hall, Inc., *Englewood Cliffs, New Jersey*

Library of Congress Cataloging in Publication Data

HORNSTEIN, HARVEY A.
  Cruelty and kindness.

  (The Patterns of social behavior series) (A
Spectrum Book)
  Includes index.
  1. Aggressiveness (Psychology) 2. Cruelty.
3. Altruism. 4. Kindness. I. Title.
BF575.A3H67   152.4   76-6911
ISBN 0-13-194928-4
ISBN 0-13-194910-1 pbk.

The Patterns of Social Behavior series
Zick Rubin, *Harvard University, General Editor*

This series brings both psychological and sociological perspectives to bear on the ways in which people affect one another. Each volume explores research on a particular aspect of social behavior and considers its personal and social implications.

©1976 by PRENTICE-HALL, INC.
Englewood Cliffs, New Jersey

A SPECTRUM BOOK

10   9   8   7   6   5   4   3   2   1

Printed in the United States of America

PRENTICE-HALL INTERNATIONAL, INC. *(London)*
PRENTICE-HALL OF AUSTRALIA PTY. LTD. *(Sydney)*
PRENTICE-HALL OF CANADA, LTD. *(Toronto)*
PRENTICE-HALL OF INDIA PRIVATE LIMITED *(New Delhi)*
PRENTICE-HALL OF JAPAN, INC. *(Tokyo)*
PRENTICE-HALL OF SOUTHEAST ASIA PTE. LTD. *(Singapore)*

Contents

Acknowledgments

I wrote this book, but many people participated in its creation. The ideas and research on which it is based were shaped and developed through the past decade by a number of friends and colleagues. Accordingly, I want to thank and praise them for their efforts.

Susan Hodgson, Hugo Masor, and Kenneth Sole were there at the beginning. They played a special role in developing the line of inquiry that led to this book. Through the years others joined them: Julie Blackman, Carol Dewey, Charles Divine, Gladys Frankel, Stephen Holloway, Sharon Kaplan, Elizabeth LaKind, Stella Manne, Janos Marton, Joyce Slochower, Janice Steil, and Lyle Tollin all contributed greatly to the final product.

For more than a decade Morton Deutsch has been my mentor, friend, and colleague. As I worked on this book, his gentle wisdom, imagination, and scholarly standards reached out from countless conversations over the years and touched every page. I am grateful and very fortunate.

My handwriting is not always legible, but Melinda Ferguson and Mildred Gude, my secretaries, cheerfully tolerated draft after draft of my scratchings, carefully deciphering my words, deletions, and inserts in order to prepare a typewritten manuscript. Some of the chapters that they typed were read and commented upon by most of the people mentioned above and also by Robert M. Krauss, Daniel McGillis, Doris Miller, Joel Seldin, Lucy Schneider, Ervin Staub, and, especially, Zick Rubin, who, along with Lynne Lumsden, provided me with important and welcome encouragement for this project.

One person who is my friend, my colleague, and my wife, Madeline Heilman, played all the roles that someone who is writing a book needs to have filled. She too was there at the beginning, and from that point onward she supported and encouraged me. She challenged my ideas and critically edited drafts of each chapter. When I was vain and grandiose she gave me humility; when I was downcast and depressed, she gave me hope. She and my daughter, Jessica, together, have allowed me to experience and understand what *we* means.

The short excerpt from the poem on page 122 appeared in Eleanor Clift, "A Singular Man: The Rising Stock of Julian Bond," *McCalls Magazine*, May 1971, p. 40. It is reprinted with permission of Julian Bond.

For permission to reprint the excerpt from "Which Side Am I Supposed to Be On?" from *Collected Shorter Poems 1927-1957* by W. H. Auden, acknowledgment is gratefully made to Random House, Inc., Faber and Faber Ltd., and Curtis Brown Ltd. Copyright 1934, renewed 1962, by W. H. Auden.

For permission to reprint the excerpt from "Anyone Lived in a Pretty How Town" from *Book of Complete Poems 1913-1962* by E. E. Cummings, acknowledgment is gratefully made to Harcourt Brace Jovanovich and Macgibbon and Kee.

HARVEY A. HORNSTEIN, Professor of Psychology and Education at Teachers College, Columbia University, maintains a consulting practice in New York City and is a senior staff member of the Center for Policy Research. A frequent contributor of research articles to professional journals, he has also co-edited *Social Intervention, The Social Technology of Organization Development,* and *Applications of Social Psychology.*

1

Neither instinct
nor aggression

All of humanity stands accused of being dominated by aggressive instincts. A primordial inheritance, these instincts are the alleged cause of both our survival as a species, and our violence, hatred, cruelty, and sadism. But in the court of scientific inquiry this accusation is being challenged by new data collected in jungles and laboratories, and on the streets of New York, Paris, and Athens. A new picture is emerging—one which suggests that the charge is erroneous and solutions based on its assumed validity are misguided.

I intend to discredit the accusation and its implications by offering in evidence psychological research which demonstrates that a fundamental aspect of human nature is man's capacity to act unselfishly. Indeed, I will argue that the very psychological structures which make aggression possible inevitably create the basis for altruism, but that neither of these two is primary or predominant. They both simply exist as parts of the human potential. Whether human beings are altruistic or aggressive, benevolent or brutal, selfless or selfish depends upon surrounding social conditions. Genes create potentials, but they do not determine social patterns. Evolution has freed us from the perniciously limiting constraints of instinct. The future is not uncontrollably embedded in our genes; it is an open book whose contents will be determined by the social conditions which we ourselves create.

This is no esoteric scientific squabble or simple academic exercise. The final verdict in this dispute will have profound social and political consequences. Even now the issues are exercising a subtle influence on social and political decision making. Many people find an appealing simplicity and some solace in the idea that aggression is instinctive. If valid, the assumption renders human behavior predictable: unconstrained, sinister desires will emerge full bloom from our ancestral depths and surround us with unbridled barbarism, war, crime, avarice, and competition. The action implication is clear. Since aggressive instincts cannot be exorcised, they must be controlled and channeled into acceptable pursuits. Society must protect and police its citizens and defend them from the presumably inevitable encroachment of other human beings. It must establish powerful arsenals in order to insure domestic and international tranquility by deterring the expression of aggressive instincts which are assumed to be a constant menace to life and liberty.

In part, the stimulus and support for these claims is the dark side of human history, which is undeniably replete with examples of human violence. Dwelling in the shadows of these events, the accusers point to the pre-eminence of aggressive instincts, and interpret human kindness, compassion, and altruism as by-products of this prime mover. By concentrating on the million, million repetitions of Cain's misdeed, they fail to understand the full message and symbolic importance of that archetypal murder.

Cain "rose up against Abel, his brother, and slew him." "See," we are told, "man's primitive aggressive instinct is supreme. It is evident even in the earliest biblical tales." But Cain's misdeed is not the whole of the story. There is another message for those who choose to read further. When the Lord inquired about Abel's whereabouts Cain said, "Am I my brother's keeper?"[1] The question is eternal. It repeatedly confronts each human being because no one's behavior is preordained to be exclusively aggressive or altruistic. Freed of instinctive shackles, we are burdened with the problem of choice.

Sometimes human beings choose to be their brother's keeper. There are times when men and women forgo trivial and significant rewards and even suffer punishment on another's behalf. They do so voluntarily, without any hope of gain for themselves. In June, 1973, for example, on three separate occasions during one seven-day period, New York City citizens unselfishly rescued their fellows from harm. With some risk to their own well-being, they protected strangers and aided in the capture of thieves and muggers. But sometimes these same New York citizens are deaf to the cries of their fellows and blind to their plight.[2]

Consider the thirty plus citizens of Kew Gardens in New York City who, some years ago, stood mute, in the safety of their homes, as one of their neighbors, Kitty Genovese, screamed for help as she was being stabbed to death. No one rushed heroically to her aid. No one shouted an alarm. No one even telephoned the police. Lament their inaction if you will, but also pause to wonder why on some occasions people act like the Good Samaritan, while on other occasions they act like the priest and the Levite who passed by that unfortunate man who lay beaten and robbed by thieves on the road that linked Jerusalem and Jericho. Why? What causes human beings to help their fellows who are in distress? When will a person act on behalf of another's goals, hopes, aspirations, and well-being?

These questions cannot be answered by appealing to instincts, aggressive or benevolent. Unlike the behavior of many subhuman species, human behavior is *not* invariant. It is, in fact, extraordinarily malleable, individually and collectively, varying enormously from time to time and place to place. Even if instincts exist in human beings, their role in determining behavior is hardly clear-cut or consistent. Nobody is aggressive or altruistic all of the time. To observe this plasticity, and then declare that every and any form of behavior and its polar opposite is a manifestation of some instinct, whether aggressive, benevolent, sexual, or territorial, is to create an explanatory fiction, fruitlessly based on tautology. Such explanations do not permit prediction. They are pragmatically worthless and scientifically unpalatable because they are unable to account adequately for the conditions which contribute to the variety and complexity of human behavior. If scientific study is to produce usable knowledge for society, then the laws of human behavior must ultimately be expressed in terms of the joint occurrence of social and psychological conditions which promote one set of behaviors or another.

Discrediting the aggressive instinct hypothesis will not be an easy task. Those who believe that human behavior is strongly influenced by a fundamental need to give vent to aggressive instincts have articulated their views with unusual clarity. And to support and illustrate their arguments they have offered as analogies to human behavior colorful examples from the antics of greylag geese, baboons, brown rats, and other subhuman species. One of the most notable members of this group is the creative scholar and Nobel prize winner, Konrad Lorenz.[3] His claim is simple: aggression is a basic instinct in both subhuman species and mankind because it has survival value. Aggression distributes animals across available territory, thereby avoiding overpopulation, and it establishes dominance and authority of the stronger over the weaker, thereby assuring a stable social structure and survival of the fittest. Contradictory as it may sound, Lorenz asserts that aggression is the basis for the formation of social bonds and personal friendships. He even goes so far as to say that". . . intraspecific aggression (author's note: aggression between members of the same species) can certainly exist without its counterpart, love, but conversely there is no love without aggression."[4]

One of the events influencing Lorenz as he was preparing to write his best seller, *On Aggression,* was a reintroduction to psychoanalytic theory. A previous exposure led Lorenz to reject aspects of psychoanalytic theory which he felt were "too audacious" and inconsistent with known biological facts. On this occasion, however, Lorenz found a compatible system of ideas. Instinctual aggression and its role in human life is one of Freud's most well-known themes. His position is set forth clearly in *Civilization and Its Discontents,* in which he writes, "Men are not gentle, friendly creatures wishing for love, who simply defend themselves if they are attacked; a powerful measure of aggression has to be reckoned as part of their instinctual endowment."[5] Freud repeatedly depicts aggression as if it were the demonic contents of a cauldron threatening to boil over, but stopped when the lid is properly fastened by parents and parental surrogates (e.g., society) whose job it is to manage and rechannel primitive drives. This view of the species *Homo sapiens* is carried beyond scientific subtlety and caution, into the extreme by Robert Ardrey, a dramatist and author of several popularized accounts of work in the natural sciences. Ardrey simply says, "Men are predators."[6]

The conclusions of scientists such as Konrad Lorenz, psychological investigators such as Sigmund Freud and Anthony Storr,[7] and popularizers of science such as Robert Ardrey and Desmond Morris[8] are part of a philosophical tradition which can be traced back at least three centuries to Thomas Hobbes.[9] A pessimist, Hobbes was so overwhelmed by what he believed to be man's uncontrollable instinctive urges that he described the natural state of mankind as "war of all against all." Variants of Hobbes's rather dismal world-view can be found in the thinking of nineteenth-century social philosophers such as Max Stirner[10] and Friedrich Nietzsche.[11] Both men proclaimed that each human being struggles for his own good, without reference to the well-being of other members of society. To exist is to struggle. There are no options. Altruism is an illusion. It is a temporary, superficial condition which exists only when people are faced by a common enemy. Bonds between men are based on common fear or common hatreds, not on love or fellowship. The struggle's roots are deep in man's past and its result is the survival of the fittest.

Superficially, the relationship between this account of social life and Darwin's analysis of human evolution seems unmistakable. During roughly the same period that Stirner and Nietzsche were laboring, a sociologist, Herbert Spencer, also observed this on-the-surface similarity. He added to it a touch of Malthusian thinking, and then proceeded to give Darwin's ideas their most comprehensive misapplication.[12]

Spencer's account of human existence is called *Social Darwinism*. Since the late 1800s, he and his followers have been arguing that the same principles which apply to the evolution and development of biological phenomena also apply to events in social life. Thus, competition between fellows is the law of life. The strongest and best survive; all the rest serve the stronger or suffer extinction. Every man is an island, each alone, pitted against his fellows in a struggle for existence. Competition, conflict, exploitation, and war are all inevitable. Moreover, they are desirable because they allow only the fittest to survive.

Although it may be unfair to hold Spencer responsible, this general theme can be found in the writings of several contemporary authors *cum* philosophers, most notably Ayn Rand.[13] One of her major complaints seems to be that societal arrangements frequently disrupt natural processes, causing some of the fit to fail and some of the unfit to survive, and even prevail. For Ms. Rand, Robin Hood was not a hero who stole from the rich and gave to the poor; he was a scoundrel who interfered with the natural course of society's evolution.

Poor Darwin, he probably never dreamed that, indirectly, his ideas would be used to attack children's heroes. In fact, they should not be. He never accepted many of the conclusions which are now being attributed to him. If one's reading of Darwin is limited to *The*

Origin of the Species, however, misinterpretation of this sort is understandable. Nevertheless, some additional effort at the library should help clarify any misconceptions. In 1871, Darwin published *The Descent of Man and Selection in Relation to Sex,* where he wrote, "As man advances in civilization and small tribes are united into larger communities, the simplest reason would tell each individual that he ought to extend his social instinct and sympathies to all members of the same nation, though personally unknown to him." This is not mere prescription. Repeatedly, throughout this book Darwin says that in nature and in human social life, cooperation and a benevolent linkage between fellows is essential for survival. In 1872, Darwin published, *The Expression of Emotion in Man and Animals,* in which he continued this argument, saying that natural selection favors the preservation of altruistic feeling, mutual aid, group loyalty, and cooperativeness. This position was echoed by a number of Darwin's contemporaries, including Prince Peter Kropotkin and anthropologist Alfred Russell Wallace, who independently formulated modern evolutionary theory contemporaneously with Darwin. Kropotkin's views are evident in the title of his classic investigation of human evolution, *Mutual Aid: A Factor of Evolution,* and Wallace stated his on March 1, 1864, in a speech delivered to the London Anthropological Society:

> In proportion as physical characteristics become of less importance, mental and moral qualities will have increasing importance to the well-being of a race. Capacity for acting in concert, for protection of food and shelter; sympathy, which leads all in turn to assist each other; the sense of right, which checks depredation. . . are all qualities that from earliest appearance must have been for the benefit of each community, and would therefore become objects of natural selection.[14]

These echoes from Darwin's time were still resounding one century later when a noted scholar, Sir Wilfred Le Gros Clark, said,

> Consciously directed cooperativeness has been the major factor which has determined the evolutionary origin of *Homo sapiens* as a new emergent species and the gradual development of the peculiarly human form of integrated society. It demanded an accelerated development of those parts of the brain whereby the emotional and instinctual impulses can be more effectively subordinated to the good of the community as a whole. Our task is to give full expression to the

deep-rooted altruism which is an essential attribute of the humanity of man.[15]

I believe that Spencer and the friends and supporters of Social Darwinism are wrong. Egoism rooted in aggressive instinct is not the rule of human life. Humans are not limited to saying "I, 'ego,' am my exclusive concern; 'we,' 'you,' and 'altruism' are shams, facades designed by the crafty and unwise to mask the ultimate truth: That all life is an *individual* struggle for existence, and maintaining *me* can be the only motive for action." I believe that self-love is *not* sovereign and human beings are *not* forever selfish, competitive, and aggressive. If there is a struggle for life, then I believe that it is often a struggle on the behalf of *another's* life.

To these biases of mine add just a few more: I believe that a final refutation of scholars such as Lorenz and Freud cannot be based simply on humanistic, philosophical, or religious commitments. And I do *not* believe that scholarly conclusions are refuted simply because one disapproves of their social and political implications. Data are needed—data collected in scientifically controlled experiments with *human beings*, data which can be used to create a new perspective for examining the literature on animal behavior. That is the content of this book. Analogies between human beings and other animals will not be primary in the development of my thesis. For illustrative purposes, I will discuss the behavior of apes, rats, porpoises, and other subhuman species, but my inferences will rest on a firm foundation of data generated by human beings, and gathered world-wide, in a great array of carefully executed experiments.

In an effort to collect these data, some scientists have spilled their groceries onto the ground in front of supermarkets in order to study bystander reaction. Others have solicited charity contributions from unsuspecting citizens, recording when people give money and when they do not. And a few have stood alongside highways for hours, waiting for some innocent motorist to stop and help them with their deliberately disabled automobiles. Incredible as it may seem, some have even lain on the floors of New York subway cars, feigning various maladies in order to study the causes of help-giving. Only a devotion to science and a deep desire to understand what motivates people to come to the aid of their fellows would compel such apparently bizarre behavior.

Reluctantly I will admit that I am unwilling to lie on the floors of New York subway cars. But I nevertheless share my colleagues' desire to understand the causes of selfless behavior. For this reason, during the past few years I have "lost" hundreds of wallets on the streets of New York City as well as several thousand contributions to different organizations, varying from charities and research foundations to self-interest groups. All this littering was done for a single purpose—to affirm, modify, and expand a theory of human behavior based on the ideas of the late Kurt Lewin, an eminent psychologist.

The data that I have collected, combined with Lewin's thoughts and the findings of other colleagues, point to a fundamentally new concept in human psychology, one which provides a scientific basis for humanist thinking. The basic ideas were identified two centuries ago by Adam Smith when he wrote, "How so ever selfish man may be supposed, there are evidently some principles in his nature which interest him in the fortune of others and render their happiness necessary to him, though he derives nothing from . . . ." One way in which this occurs is ". . . by changing places with the sufferer, so that we come either to conceive or be affected by what he feels." In these words Adam Smith recorded his observation of man's capacity for unselfish behavior and acknowledged that it was probably facilitated by a kind of empathic state.[16]

Psychological investigations involving ten thousand and more human beings have confirmed Adam Smith's insights: on some occasions, human beings experience a sense of community, a feeling of oneness with their fellows. When that happens the words of John Donne's seventeenth "Devotion" are given their fullest meaning:

> No man is an *Island,* entire of itself; every man is a piece of the *Continent,* a part of the *main;* if a *Clod* be washed away by the *Sea, Europe* is the less, as well as if a Manor of *thy* friends or of thine *own* were; any man's death diminishes *me,* because I am involved in *Mankind;* and therefore never send to know for whom the *bell* tolls; it tolls for thee.

As the famed sociologist Charles Horton Cooley once wrote, "Perhaps the simpliest way of describing this wholeness is by saying it is a 'we'. . . . It involves the sort of sympathy and mutual identification for which 'we' is the natural expression."[17] On some occasions, social conditions cause human beings to experience each other as *we,* not *they.* When this happens bonds exist which permit one person's plight to become a source of tension for his fellows. I will call it *promotive tension.* Unconsciously seeking relief, they reduce this tension by aiding a fellow "*we*-grouper." *Hedonism compels altruism*, and it is transformed in the process. In forming *we*-groups, men are joined with their fellows and some distinctions between self and other are transcended. When another with whom one is in union needs aid, then self-interest is served and tension is reduced when one acts on the other's behalf. Through the formation of *we*, self-interest is fused together with a concern for others, and the basis of promotive tension and selfless behavior is born.

The formation of *we* is the next chapter's principal concern. As I have suggested, genes create potentials, but they do not determine human social patterns. The second chapter ("We and They") examines the many ways in which bonds of *we* and barriers of *they* are erected and eroded by social forces, causing the occurrence of both human kindness and cruelty.

In chapters three and four, childhood experience and the last few million years of human evolution are both identified as contributors to our individual readiness for experiencing both empathy and the bonds of *we*. Chapter three ("Early Childhood Experiences: Into the Minds of Babes") explores how social development and child-rearing experiences affect the realization of our potential for engaging in selfless behavior. And chapter four ("Human Evolution: A Hunting We Will Go") investigates the way in which a prehistoric dependence on cooperative social organization necessarily exerted a selective force on human evolution in the direction of developing abstract thought, empathy, and an ability to experience bonds of *we* and barriers of *they*. It concludes that because ideas, not instincts, guide the formation of these social ties, human beings are potentially the cruelist and kindest animals on earth.

Human capacity for benevolence is extraordinary, but it is not unique. Infrahuman species are not without an ability to act kindly toward members of their species. But as you will learn in chapter five ("Infrahuman Animals and Altruism: Everybody's Doin' It"), identifying what is and what is not true altruism among these species is difficult. They do not respond to interviewer's questions, nor are they facile in completing questionnaires. And interpretation of data gleaned by observation of their antics is filled with pitfalls born of human subjectivity. These issues are discussed in chapter five and experimental evidence is offered to demonstrate that infrahuman primates, and probably other species as well, are more disposed to act altruistically toward *we* rather than *they*.

Why the bonds of *we* produce altruism and kindness, while the barriers of *they* suppress such humane behavior, is the concern of chapters six ("A Small Cafe in Berlin") and seven ("Promotive Tension: A Tree Grows in Brooklyn"). In these chapters I discuss some aspects of the psychology of selflessness. Evidence is presented which indicates that human beings experience an inner tension upon witnessing the plight of others with whom they are united in *we*, and, for relief, they act on the other's behalf. Chapter eight ("Ties that Bind") presents further evidence concerning the consequences of experiencing bonds of *we*, and analyzes the social conditions which cause the creation of these bonds among human beings. Attention is given to events in Bristol and Brooklyn, and Paris, Athens, and Boston, all of which have served as settings for systematic scientific inquiry aimed at identifying principles which describe the circumstances that cause one human being to encounter another and feel "You and I are *We*."

The remaining chapters are concerned with our society and the way in which it builds and destroys the ties that bind. Human beings inevitably have the capacity for selfless, caring behavior, but society must work to create the social conditions which activate this capacity. Chapter nine ("Some News is Good News") presents evidence which proves that morning news, which is filled with tales of humanity's most noble and villainous deeds, may influence listeners, later in the day, to either help strangers who are in need of aid, or turn away apathetically.

Chapter ten ("Deindividuation: Losing the *Me* and the *You*") is concerned with deindividuation of self and others. This chapter asks whether the social apathy and callously inhumane irresponsibility that we bemoan in contemporary society reflect the effect of deindividuation on *we*-group ties. When social conditions deny us a sense of individual identity, there is no *me*. When they cause us to pigeon-hole others into categories and deny them their individual identity, there is no *you*. Without a clear, affirmative sense of *me* and *you*, there can be no *we*. The tragic consequence makes newspaper headlines. Submerged in the anomie and alienation of our society, all too often we are psychologically deaf to the pleading of others. More and more, help-giving seems to be reserved for the few, and in response to the plight of many we witness only apathy and self-concern. The condition is tragic but not irrevocable. *We*-group ties are not inflexible. If they have been narrowed in these past few decades, then they can be broaded again. The eleventh and concluding chapter ("Where Will We Go?") discusses why changing social conditions may help to establish *we*-group ties so that we will never again have cause to wonder for whom the bell tolls.

Notes

1. Genesis, chapter 4, verse 8, *The Dartmouth Bible.*

2. One of these events is reported in *The New York Times,* Sunday, June 17, 1973, p. 31. The other two occurred within the next few days and were reported on WINS, a local radio news station in New York City.

3. Konrad Lorenz, *On Aggression* (New York: Bantam Books, Inc., 1967).

4. Ibid, p. 209.

5. Sigmund Freud, *Civilization and Its Discontents* (London: Hogarth Press, 1927), p. 85.

6. Robert Ardrey, *African Genesis* (New York: Antheum, 1961).

7. Anthony Storr, *Human Aggression* (London: Penguin Books Ltd., 1968); also, Anthony Storr, *Human Destructiveness* (New York: Basic Books, Inc., Publishers, 1972).

8. Desmond Morris, *The Naked Ape* (New York: McGraw-Hill Book Company, 1967).

9. Thomas Hobbes (1851), *Leviathan* (New York: The Bobbs-Merrill Co., Inc., 1958).

10. Max Stirner (1845), *The Ego and His Own* (New York: B. R. Tucker, 1907).

11. Oscar Levy, ed., *The Complete Works of Friedrich Nietzsche* (Edinburgh and London: T. N. Foulis, 1910).

12. Herbert Spencer, *First Principles* (New York: D. Appleton & Co., 1864); *The Principles of Ethics* (New York: D. Appleton & Co., 1895–98); also, Herbert Spencer, *The Principles of Sociology,* 3 vols. (New York: D. Appleton & Co., 1876–97).

13. Ayn Rand, *The Fountainhead,* 25th anniversary edition (New York: The Bobbs-Merrill, Co., Inc., 1968); Ayn Rand, *Atlas Shrugged* (New York: Random House, Inc., 1957).

14. Quoted by Robert Ardrey, in *The Territorial Imperative* (New York: Dell Publishing Co., 1966), pp. 261–62.

15. From a presidential address and quoted in John Lewis and Bernard Towers, *Naked Ape or Homo Sapiens* (New York: New American Library, Inc., Mentor Books, 1972); see also W. E. LeGros Clark, *Man-apes or Ape-men?* (New York: Holt, Rinehart & Winston, Inc., 1967).

16. Adam Smith, *The Theory of Moral Sentiments* (1759) in H. Schneider, ed.,

Adam Smith's Moral and Political Philosophy (New York: Hafner Publishing Co., Inc., 1948).

17. Charles Horton Cooley, *Social Organization* (New York: Scribner, 1909).

2

We and they

Senator Sam Ervin's gavel descended, the United States Senate investigation of Watergate began, and for two days in June, 1973, Mr. Herbert L. Porter occupied stage center. Mr. Porter was a Watergate fatality. He was involved. He was also young, only thirty-five, and his position in the Committee for the Re-election of the President gained him little notoriety. He was its scheduling director. Alongside the testimony given by such superstars as Mitchell, Ehrlichman, and Halderman, Mr. Porter's threatens to pass easily from public recollection. But that should not happen. He said things that capture both the psychology of that deplorable episode and the special circumstances that fostered its occurrence. In describing his first days as a White House staff member, Mr. Porter said, "There definitely did exist a 'we-they' attitude. 'We' being anyone inside the gate, 'they' being all others, particularly the press, and of course the opposition party. On my first or second day in the White House, Dwight Chapin said to me, 'One thing you should realize early on, we are practically an island here.' That is the way the world was viewed."[1]

Mr. Porter's statement suggests that this view of the world began with his participation in the Nixon Administration. Unfortunately for Mr. Porter, a person's view of who is *we* and who is *they* is not fixed. It changes as each of us is captured in a continuous swirl of human events.

When They Make Us Into We

Without another word about Mr. Porter's testimony and its relevance to we-group formation and promotive tension, I want to tell you a story about Halloween, and then share with you a quote from Konrad Lorenz. Connections between Mr. Porter's statement and these two bits of material will emerge; that I guarantee.

Young boys and girls (and a few grown-up ones, as well) are often frightened by what is not there. "It," "them," and horrible hidden things produce frights that are often remembered long into adulthood. A very special night for such scares is Halloween. For some youngsters, Halloween is that time of year when things that go bump in the night, bump with unusual terror and reality.

Several years ago, a group of boys, ages nine to twelve, were telling ghost stories at a Halloween party—tales from the crypt, involving things that creep, scream, and rattle, and deformed, deranged beings that lurk in shadows and dwell in dark forests. Sitting in a circle, they told their horror stories, one after another. And as they did, the circle grew smaller and smaller, moving from a diameter of eleven feet to approximately three feet.[2] Frightened of *them*, these boys literally moved closer toward *we*. Konrad Lorenz[3] tells us, "As far as I know, there is not a single gregarious animal species whose individuals do not press together when alarmed, that is, whenever there is suspicion that a predator is close at hand."

Real or imagined threats from *them*, can enhance we-group solidarity. Indeed, it can even produce bonds where none existed. Jamaica, a community in Queens, New York, for example, was not known for its neighborhood spirit. Its story is typical: older residents—lower middle-class to middle-class whites; newer residents—lower middle-class to middle-class blacks; history—trouble. But on one Sunday in May, 1973, Mother's Day, a tragic event occurred which temporarily formed residents into a we-group whose members cared about one other.

Sometime after services had ended, Father Conlin was counting the contributions. The parish was not in a very wealthy area, and the contributions, which must have meant so much to the parishioners, were not very great, only four hundred dollars, in total. Father

Conlin himself, by all accounts, was a simple, unassuming man. Earthy and kind, he was devoted to his parish. These thoughts were tragically evident in the tears shed by young and old, black and white, and male and female who wept openly upon hearing that someone murdered this gentle human being in order to steal the Mother's Day collection. The neighborhood mourned, and a few days later, at the Father's funeral, John Lindsey, the Mayor of New York City, expressed sorrow and horror at the tragedy, but also observed that one good thing may have emerged during the period of distress: differences were set aside by the residents as everyone worked cooperatively.[4] One or more unknown marauders crept into the neighborhood, violated its sanctity and, for a moment, caused strangers to stand side-by-side providing each other with aid and comfort. Because of *them*, out of *you* and *I*, emerged *we*.

During the summers of 1949, 1953, and 1954 an unusually typical group of American boys, ages eleven and twelve, attended camps where they unknowingly participated in several psychological investigations which have a bearing on this process of *we*-group formation. Prior screening of these youngsters insured that they satisfied several criteria: they were strangers to one another, middle-class or lower middle-class, and Protestant. None came from broken homes, and their I.Q.'s were slightly above average. They were normal, healthy, and without any severe problems of social adjustment. Yet, after only a short time at camp, they were involved in a hostile and heated *us* vs. *them* conflict that was deliberately created and then resolved by a social psychologist, Muzafer Sherif, and his associates.[5] "The conflict was relatively easy to create," said Sherif. "A series of situations was introduced in which one group could achieve its goal only at the expense of the other group. . . . The results of this stage of intergroup conflict supported our main hypothesis. During interaction between groups (in activities). . . which were competitive and mutually frustrating, members of each group developed hostile attributes and highly unfavorable stereotypes toward the other group and its members. In fact, attitudes of social distance between the groups became so definite that they wanted to have nothing further to do with each other."

These boys were not characteristically aggressive. Prior to this experiment hostility and anger were in no way predominant or excessive in their repertoire. Their behavior before and during the experiment cannot be explained in terms of strict biological determinism or personality. Social conditions, in this instance created by a clever social psychologist, caused these boys to divide their small summer world into *we* and *they*, and aggress against their fellows. Parallels can be established between this small experiment and the behavior of larger groups.

During the seventeenth century the Iroquois became a highly warlike military nation.[6] But they were not always so. Prior to contact with Europeans, they were a hunting people with a subsistence economy. Europeans brought with them the possibility of trade. Furs could be exchanged for metal tools, guns, and other manufactured items. Unfortunately, the Iroquois depleted their forests more rapidly than they exhausted their desire for European trade goods. Their desire for these items, which by this point can be more accurately described as a dependence, brought them into direct competition with surrounding Indian tribes, especially the Huron, who also coveted fur, and the trade possibilities its possession bestowed. War began. But not because the Iroquois were unable to contain aggressive instincts. The historical pattern is clear. Like Sherif's summer campers, changing social conditions caused their aggressive behavior. And, as in the case of Sherif's summer campers, changing social conditions, not the satisfaction of instinctual drives, caused hostilities to cease.

Several strategies were employed by Sherif in order to resolve the conflict among his feuding summer campers. One of the more colorful and illuminating failures was a "goodwill" dinner which brought the warring factions together. Unfortunately, the dinner only served as a vehicle for continuing the conflict. Food proved to be a particularly good missile for hurtling at one's enemy.

Two other tactics of conflict resolution were more successful. Both illustrate how *they* make *us* into *we*. One, the *common enemy approach*, was effective in uniting some groups in common cause against other groups. "But," as Sherif said, "bringing some groups together against others means larger and more devastating conflicts in the long run." Another, more promising method, was called the *super-ordinate goal approach*. It required the warring groups to cooperate in order to attain certain desired goals. For example, one morning the camp's water pipeline was broken and could not be repaired unless everyone joined in the effort. On another day, a truck that was supposed to bring lunch to the boys, who had been hiking, broke down. Unless they all joined together, by pulling a rope, the truck would be unable to start.

Events like these were not like the goodwill dinner. They did not simply involve contact between the groups. Rather, they involved cooperative interaction in order to attain goals which could not be achieved by one group's efforts. The effect of these joint activities was to reduce hostility and lessen ingroup-outgroup distinctions. One group emerged where before there existed feuding factions.

Breeders of wild geese, of all people, have recognized the manner in which *they* make *we* out of *us*. Breeders of wild geese, you see, rely upon the geese to do the breeding. Sometimes the geese's romantic interests and a breeder's financial ones are not harmonious, and two potentially promising parents refuse to mate. One solution to this obstinacy is to relocate the two in an unfamiliar group. As the new goose and gander in town, they are not warmly welcomed by the older residents. Separated from others, and cast into a common group, they only have one another and. . . .[7]

Just like politics, under some circumstances, *they* can make strange bedfellows. In fact, a literal interpretation of this statement is not too far beyond the realm of scientific evidence. An investigation, published in a 1972 issue of the *Journal of Personality and Social Psychology,* reported a phenomenon labeled the "Romeo and Juliet effect."[8] Shakespeare's famous lovers, you will recall, were from two feuding families, the Montagues and Capulets, which caused them much grief, but in no way dampered their love. So it was with 140 couples who participated in this investigation. After examining the data, the three investigating psychologists concluded: "These results, when taken together, provide strong support for the causal hypothesis that parental opposition leads to romantic love."

The ties that bound these lovers together, like the ties that bound the breeders' geese, Sherif's summer campers, Jamaica's residents, and President Nixon's staff were partially contingent on the perception of outside events, the social context. Whether I believe that *you* and *I* are *we*, can depend upon who *they* are and what *they* are doing.

In his book, *Folkways,* William Graham Sumner wrote, "The exigencies of war with outsiders are what make peace inside, lest internal discord should weaken the we-group for war. These exigencies also make government and law in the in-group, in order to prevent quarrels and enforce discipline."[9] When hazards threaten, one's interest and welfare are sometimes interlocked with the interests and welfare of others. As the target of a common enemy, you and I become *we*. Our differences are minimized and our similarities are exaggerated. But to our views of *them* quite the opposite occurs. Attempts are made to create the widest psychological gap as differences are exaggerated and similarities are minimized.[10] The ultimate consequence of this cycle is familiar, and needs no elaboration: affection for *we* increases, as does antagonism toward *they*. Strengthened in this way, *we-they* distinctions provide the basis for waging war against *they* and self-sacrifice on behalf of *we*.

If what I am saying leads you to conclude that either enmity or external hazard is essential for the formation of *we*-groups quickly do whatever is necessary to eliminate that falsehood from your thinking. In his book, *The Territorial Imperative*, Robert Ardrey makes this very mistake. He concludes that amity is a function of enmity and hazard. He even offers a little illustrative formula: $A = E + h$. But enmity between fellows is *not* an essential condition for amity. Hazard is not required for *you* and *I* to become *we*. The true relationship between amity and enmity, and *we* and *they*, was recognized by the late Gordon W. Allport, in his classic work, *The Nature of Prejudice:* ". . . although we could not perceive our own in-groups excepting as the contrast to out-groups, still the in-groups are psychologically primary. We live in them, by them, and, sometimes, for them. Hostility toward out-groups helps strengthen our sense of belonging, but is not required."[11] Amity and enmity, and *we-* and *they*-group formation are reciprocal capacities in human and subhuman species. "Discriminative aggression toward strangers and the bond between members of a group enhance each other," says Konrad Lorenz.[12] Undoubtedly, each of these capacities is spotlighted and stimulated by the other's existence, but neither *requires* the other for its formation. *They* can create *we*. But feelings of *we*, like feelings of *they*, can spring forth independently, as a natural response to one's fellows.

The Tasaday, a recently discovered people who live in Philippine rain forests have had no human enemies for hundreds of years. The word *war* is not in their language.[13] Yet amity, feelings of *we* prevail. For *you* and *I* to become *we*, *they* need not be hostile or threatening.

Dr. Harvey Allen demonstrated this in an investigation that involved unsuspecting subway riders in New York City.[14] Have you ever ridden the New York subways? No experience is quite the equivalent. As a native New Yorker it pains me to admit that traveling by subway is not as easy as it might be. The city's size is certainly one problem. It is a large subway system that serves millions of riders. Such scale of operation requires complexity. But one would hope that necessity is the mother of invention, and that the need for complexity would bring forth creatively composed, easily understood travel information. Alas, that has not happened. Most of the information is phrased in the language of intelligence test questions: "The QQ train to Kew Gardens does not stop at 40th Avenue except between 7 P.M. and 3 A.M. Monday–Friday. Take the DD downtown to 10th Street, change to the uptown L, which makes all express stops except holidays and weekends." And the maps, abundant as they are, seem to me a tribute to the influence of Jackson Pollack. Under such circumstances, is it any wonder that people wander around these subterranean chambers, hopelessly lost, desperately needing aid? This was the plight of a young man in the investigation conducted by Dr. Harvey Allen.

After entering a subway car, this young man, in reality one of Allen's associates, looked puzzled and approached two passengers, one of whom was a fraud, another of Allen's confederates. Above the roar and rattle of the train, which was by now heading *uptown,* the young man asked, "Is this train heading downtown?" Sometimes, in an obvious manner, his question was addressed to the unsuspecting commuter. At other times it was addressed either to the other confederate, directly, or to the surrounding group, but no one in particular. All this was irrelevant to Allen's other confederate, who immediately answered the young man's question with a loud, incorrect, "Yes." Now, fully informed with the wrong information, the young man sat down nearby. Shortly afterward the bogus commuter who so willingly provided misinformation left. Question: when will the innocent bystander intervene to correct the mistaken instructions? When will he or she care enough to help this innocent victim reach his goal?

Place yourself in the innocent bystander's position. When would you feel most directly connected with the young man? Almost everyone who has answered this question for me has said, "when he spoke directly to me."

Mr. or Ms. N.Y. Subway Rider felt the same way. They intervened most often when the young man created ties by addressing the inquiry directly to them: On those occasions 96.67 percent eventually spoke up and corrected the misinformation. When the inquiry was addressed to the other stooge or to the group, and there was no link between Mr. or Ms. N.Y. Subway Rider and this hapless young man, many fewer came to his aid. In each instance, only 53.33 percent bothered to correct the young man's faulty travel plans. Unless ties were created by a direct plea for help, Mr. or Ms. N.Y. Subway

Rider left the young man to suffer the consequences of his misfortune.

That is regrettable, but the gloom it casts should not mask an important implication of this investigation: *we* was created in the absence of threats from *they*, and no hazard existed to fuse *you* and *I* into *we*. Ties were established and help was given simply because one human being actively invited another to become responsible for his welfare. Passengers who initially regarded this young man as neither *we* nor *they*, accepted this relationship and responded: nearly 100 percent became their brother's keeper.

My Brother's Keeper

Baboon troops have leaders who are also baboons. When confronted with external threats such as other baboon troops, predators, and human handlers, leader baboons will often risk serious dangers to protect those in their care from harm. One baboon leader, described by DeVore and Hall,[15] for example, spent much of his time being a tyrant. He fornicated with any and all females in estrus, drove the lesser males away, and was very accustomed to having subordinate males "present" to him, that is, approach him as a supplicant, in a manner similar to a female in heat. But on one occasion, when an eland cow charged the troop, this leader behaved admirably. He did not run or pressure subordinate males into the front ranks. Instead, he stood his ground allowing others to retreat. Surely this baboon, and others of his kind, could do otherwise without fear of a baboon court-martial. They rule primarily through strength, not reputation. Whatever compels them to protect their fellows, it does not derive from a fear of being called "coward"; rather it is associated with the role that they occupy.

Human beings also assume responsibility for others' welfare because of the role they occupy. Can you recollect your early days in primary school? Somehow my memories of those days are always flooded with remembrances of odors, the glue that we used, crayons, paints, the wax on too-warm containers of milk. And, of course, I remember those times when I was asked to be a monitor, which was not terribly often in my case. Being responsible for others is a very important and adult event for children. Professor Ervin A. Staub once conducted an investigation of the behavior of children who were "left in charge."

In his experiment,[16] some first graders were left in charge of a group and were told to "take care of things" while an adult was away. Others were left alone, but without being given any such responsibility. After a few moments, sounds of a child in distress suddenly came *from an adjoining room.* Of course, these noises were fabricated for the sole purpose of observing and comparing the responses of youngsters with and without assigned responsibility. Children who were "in charge" were very likely to attempt to leave the room in order to help. The others, who were not given the role of "caretaker" or "leader," but who heard the same sounds, were not nearly so likely to make this attempt. The other's plight was not their concern. Before discussing why this difference in behavior occurred, let us turn to a related investigation by Dr. Harvey A. Tilker.[17]

"This is an investigation of the relationship between punishment and learning," participants in his study were told, falsely. A rigged lottery caused each of these participants to occupy the role of *observer.* Two other people who were also there, both Tilker's confederates, occupied the roles of *teacher* and *learner.* Whenever the learner gave a correct response to the teacher's question, all went well, and the teacher proceeded with a new question. For every incorrect response, however, Tilker told the teacher to punish the learner with an electric shock, and, he added, increase it fifteen volts for each incorrect answer until the learner succeeds, or receives 375 volts, whichever comes first.

The observer's role in this potentially painful interchange varied. Some observers had *no responsibility,* and were told, "You two (that is, the observer and teacher) may discuss anything you wish, however, *the teacher has complete responsibility* for the conduct of the study as well as *the well-being of the learner* [italics are mine], and his decisions on procedural matters will be final. I will be in my office next door." Other observers were given *ambiguous responsibility;* they were told:

> You two may discuss anything you wish and resolve all procedural differences between yourselves. I will be in my office next door.

And, one final group of observers were given *total responsibility:*

> You two may discuss anything you wish, however, since you are in the best position to judge developments as they might occur, *you will*

be responsible for the study as well as *the well-being of the learner.* (Italics are mine). Your decisions on procedural matters will be final. I will be in my office next door.

When the learner's feigned ordeal began, he was separated from the observer and teacher, who were together. Sometimes the separation was total and the observer and teacher were completely cut off from the learner's anguish and protest; there was no auditory or visual contact. Some observers and teachers had only auditory contact; they could hear the learner's cries and pleading, but he was otherwise hidden from view. And others could both see and hear the learner as he protested and his body convulsed each time electric current ripped through him. Of course, all this was staged for the observer's benefit.

Question: When did the observer object? When did he interfere and prevent the learner from suffering excessive harm? Answer: An observer was most likely to object and stop the teacher when he had *total responsibility* and both auditory and visual contact.[18] As Tilker says:

> All the [people] in this condition made significantly more verbal protests, and they tended to do so earlier in the sequence of experimental events. All of them stopped the experiment and they did so significantly earlier than other [people] who stopped the experiment. In addition, at a point at which most subjects in other conditions were just beginning to verbally protest, or were still protesting, the maximum feedback and total responsibility subjects were stopping the experiment. . . .[19]

Being bound to the other because of the responsibility inherent in one's position was insufficient to motivate helping. Being completely exposed to the other's desperation was also insufficient. Both were essential to produce action. Observers became "friends indeed" when they were confronted with irrefutable evidence of the learner's plight *and* when they were assigned responsibility for being their brother's keeper. Ties created by assigned responsibility were essential, but they produced little help when another's plight could be denied or distorted.[20]

Unlike Allen's subway riders, Tilker's observers and Staub's monitors had their roles assigned to them. Their responsibility for others' welfare was detailed in reasonably explicit terms. Just why they helped cannot be pinpointed, but three nonmutually exclusive possibilities seem evident. First, Staub's and Tilker's participants may have viewed helping as a tacit job requirement. From this perspective, they were just fulfilling an obligation out of a sense of duty, much as police and firemen do. Their behavior was impersonal and motivated by unwritten job requirements. Second, it is possible that Staub's monitors and Tilker's observers differed from their counterparts because their jobs provided the kind of authority that allowed them to initiate uncustomary behavior in a strange, unstructured situation. Young children do not ordinarily make unauthorized departures from their assigned rooms in school buildings, and participants in experiments, young or old, rarely see themselves as having the authority to unilaterally stop the experiment. Perhaps the authority invested in monitors' and observers' roles allowed their occupants to behave in ways that were psychologically forbidden to their counterparts who occupied no such role.

Third, the roles occupied by Staub's monitors and Tilker's observers may have created an altered sense of responsibility for the welfare of others. Thus, helping was prompted because the job assigned to these participants heightened their awareness of a commonly voiced social rule: we ought to help our fellows who are in need of aid. Separately or together, these three possibilities may account for the behavior of Staub's and Tilker's participants, but they are not applicable to the behavior of Allen's subway riders.

Passengers who helped the young man were not conductors or transit patrolmen; they did not occupy any special role prior to the critical event. They were simply Mr. or Ms. New York Subway Rider. When the young man approached, looked directly at them and said, "Is this train going downtown?", responsibility for his welfare was unexpectedly thrust upon them. It was as if he said, "*My* welfare is in *your* hands!" His plea was *focused* and *invitational;* it was *not* a *demand* for aid.[21] It changed a commuter's relationship to this young man. To each other they were no longer completely anonymous strangers, one among many indistinguishable faces in a crowd. A needy supplicant, who was *not* a *they,* invited them, particularly, to provide aid, and, for a moment, special ties were created. A temporary and probably precarious social unit formed, and the previously amorphous, undifferentiated crowd was divided into two groups: *we* ("the guy who asked for my help and me") and everyone else.

The conjunction of two events motivated Mr. or Ms. N.Y. Subway

Rider to help the young man. He was needy and he directed his plea for help directly at them. Throughout the animal kingdom there are examples of how blatant and focused displays of helplessness and dependency inhibit attacks from members of the same species. Displays of vulnerability directed at a particular other is the essence of appeasing gestures among many subhuman species. Dogs roll on their backs, exposing their vulnerable undersides. And water rail chicks perform appeasing gestures with the aid of a small organ called the *corpus covernosum*, which is mounted on top of their skulls. Gorged with blood, it provides a fine red signal. By presenting the tops of their skulls, which are soft and vulnerable, but nicely red, chicks inhibit fatal pecking attacks from larger water rails.[22]

Humans are no less responsive to dependency on the part of someone who is not a *they*. Dr. Elizabeth Midlarsky,[23] for example, found that a person handicapped by broken eyeglasses received more aid from their partner than one whose eyeglasses were intact, but whose task-related needs were exactly the same. This was so despite the fact that giving aid yielded no tangible benefit to the helper and, in fact, required them to undergo unpleasant electric shock! To this investigation add nearly one dozen more conducted by Professor Leonard Berkowitz of the University of Wisconsin.[24] These investigations have repeatedly demonstrated that in many circumstances helping and dependency go hand-in-hand.

But human responses to dependency are not instinctively compelled. They depend on social circumstance. Commonplace experience forces us to recognize that those who are more fortunate do not inevitably have unbounded benevolent concern for helpless, dependent supplicants. History books and contemporary newspaper headlines provide too many accounts of the exploitation of needy people by an elite who regards them as irrevocably inferior, as *they*. Dependency produces helping only when the other is not clearly a *they*. This was nicely illustrated by two friends of mine, Professor Bibb Latane of Ohio State University and Professor John M. Darley of Princeton University.[25] They once sent their students into the streets in order to solicit funds from passersby. "Excuse me, can you spare a. . . " But there was a twist. Sometimes these bogus panhandlers were neatly attired; at other times the very same people were shabby looking. When did the passersby, who were average citizens, help most often? Can there be any doubt? In shabby dress, the bogus panhandlers were *they*, and fewer people provided help.

Man's concern with being his brother's keeper is an ancient one. It pervades literature, philosophy, and religion. One relevant story in the Bible which I particularly like is the tale of Jonah and the whale. Most people seem to know that Jonah was consumed by a whale. But fewer know why Jonah ended up in the big fellow's gastrointestinal tract and what happened to him afterward.

In Jonah's day there was a city called Nineveh. The Bible tells us that this city had a goodly number of cattle and sixscore thousand (120,000) people who could not discern between their right and left hands. Apparently, this population of dullards had a propensity for the kind of evil behavior which offended God. Being in a particularly benevolent mood, however, God withheld immediate punishment, and told Jonah to warn the Ninevites that penalties would be forthcoming if they failed to mend their ways. The task created a dilemma for Jonah. He did not want to help, and, in fact, he hoped to see the Ninevites punished. He certainly must have regarded these profligate folk as *they*. After all, defying a request from God is no small matter. Instead of delivering His warning, Jonah tried to run away. The escape was thwarted by the now-famous whale who included Jonah in his diet for the day.

The symbolism here is especially apt. Jonah, who felt no solidarity or responsibility for his fellows in Nineveh, answered "No" to the unasked, but ever-present question "Am I my brother's keeper?" and ended up alone, isolated and imprisoned in the stomach of the world's largest mammal. By excluding a part of humanity from his *we*-group, he was excluded from humanity.

God eventually rescued Jonah, who carried out the mission. Nineveh was saved, which upset Jonah since he was still ignorant of the moral of the story in which he plays so prominent a part. Once again God punished him. This time by taking away a shade tree that Jonah favored. Poor Jonah, he stupidly complained to God about the loss of his shade tree, whereupon God gave him a stern, to-the-point lecture, which we can assume had the intended effect.

Jonah is passengers on a train and children at school. He is a citizen of Brooklyn, Bristol, Paris, and Athens. Jonah is all of us. For reasons great and small, we classify others as *they*, and to the question "Am I my brother's keeper?" we answer, "No," frequently risking more than the loss of a shade tree.

Race and the Ties That Bind.

I want to tell you four short stories. All of them have very nearly the same ending.

One December, in Trenton, New Jersey, 3,703 shoppers (2,154 women and 1,549 men) were given the opportunity to provide the Salvation Army with a Christmas contribution. Two kettles stood in a shopping area, seventy-five yards apart. Both were attended by females, one white and one black. Periodically, they switched locations, so that neither was by one kettle all the time. No gestures were made; no requests for donations were voiced. They just stood alongside the kettles, patiently waiting for Christmastime acts of charity. Those acts occurred, but in considerably greater number for the white than for the black Salvation Army worker. The shoppers were white.[26]

Five hundred sixty-nine residents of Brooklyn, New York were at home when their telephone suddenly rang. "Hello." "Hello." (Pause.) "Ralph's Garage. . . " It was obviously a wrong number. "No, this isn't Ralph's Garage." Now the caller's situation changed from difficult to tragic. Quickly he explained that he was stuck on the highway, away from anywhere, without a second dime to make another telephone call. This message confronted some of Brooklyn's fine citizens with yet another dilemma: should they help this fellow by calling his garage, or should they hang up and forget the whole affair? One other detail: half of the calls were made by blacks, deliberately effecting a "modified southern Negro" dialect. The other half were made by whites. Sixty-five percent of the white callers and fifty-three percent of the black callers were helped. The people whose telephones brought them this plea for aid were white.[27]

Late in the spring of 1968, approximately four thousand passengers who rode the New York subway's IND train between 59th and 125th streets were witness to an almost tragic sight. A man, who entered the train at 59th Street, staggered and collapsed to the floor. To lie on the floor of a New York subway car, which is indescribably filthy, one must be truly sick, a psychological researcher, or both. Fortunately, this fellow's collapse was completely contrived and solely for the purpose of psychological research. He and his less conspicuous confederates, who were sitting in the car disguised as ordinary passengers, were concerned with identifying who helped and how quickly help was forthcoming.

Matters were made more interesting by having not one victim, but four. Of course, they did not all flop to the floor on the same occasion. Instead, riders witnessed just one of the victims in his award-winning performance. The victim was either white or black, and was either sober, carrying a cane, or drunk.

Once again New Yorkers disproved the maligning stereotype of their heartlessness. They helped with determination and vigor. Sixty-two of the sixty-five cane victims and nineteen of the thirty-eight drunk victims received spontaneous help, and much of the time, help came from more than one person. But this isn't the whole story. The subway cars were populated by whites and blacks in approximately equal numbers. Of the eighty-one people who provided spontaneous help, sixty-four percent helped victims of the same race, but only thirty-six percent helped victims of another race.[28]

Supermarket shopping is not one of life's peak moments. Imagine yourself trying to push through narrow aisles with a cart that insists on veering to the left, often into the heels of innocent shoppers who are stooped over, studying undecipherable information about the unit cost of tuna fish. Finally, your shopping completed, you pay, take your purchases, leave the store, and, as you enter the parking lot, your shopping bag splits wide open. A fitting end to a morning of shopping.

Professor Lauren G. Wispé and his associate Harold Freshley conducted an investigation which exploited this everyday tragedy.[29] They call their experiment "The Broken Bag Caper." For twelve weekends, on Friday evenings, and Saturday mornings and afternoons, these two scientists conducted their experiment at various shopping centers located in a southwestern city in the United States. The 176 black and white, male and female shoppers involved in this investigation witnessed the event I just described: another shopper's bag of groceries split open, emptying its contents to the ground. The event was staged, and the victim of this mishap, who was either white or black, male or female, was Wispé's and Freshley's confederate.

Passing shoppers had a choice: They could provide *no help* by simply continuing on their way; they could provide *perfunctory help* by picking up a few groceries and then moving along; or they could provide what these two investigators called *positve help* by helping with all the groceries, offering to get a new bag, or the like.

Black passersby provided blacks with help in the following proportions: *positive help*, 20 percent; *perfunctory help*, 18 percent; *no help*, 62 percent. To whites they provided slightly less help, but the differences are very small indeed: *positive help*, 18 percent; *perfunctory help*, 14 percent; *no help*, 68 percent.

White passersby present a more complicated picture, but one that contains a familiar, unsatisfying theme: When the victim was also white 27 percent provided *positive help*, 16 percent *perfunctory help*, and 57 percent *no help*. When the victim was black, however, only 13 percent provided *positive help*, but 32 percent provided *perfunctory help*, and 55 percent *no help*.[30] Overall, blacks helped others somewhat less frequently than whites, but they did so almost without regard to race. Whites, however, provided other whites with decidedly more enthusiastic helping then they provided blacks.

This was the final story in the quartet. The ending is familiar: same-race helping tends to predominate. But this last story brings into sharper focus an aberration in the quartet's theme: the same-race helping pattern seems more characteristic of whites than blacks. Parts of the other stories, which I previously neglected to mention, support this observation.

On New York subway cars, when the victim with a cane collapsed, race was critical only to whites. Blacks, in fact, show a slight tendency toward helping white victims more frequently. Even when another needed aid because he was drunk, the tendency to help a victim of the same race was more pronounced among whites than blacks.

You read about what occurred when 569 white Brooklynites received a telephone call intended for Ralph's Garage: they helped white callers more frequently than black ones. What I neglected to say is that there were 540 *black* Brooklynites who received that same telephone call. They did not show any tendency to help same-race victims. On the contrary, there was once again a slight tendency to help whites more frequently. A pattern is emerging: blacks tended to show either no preference or a slight preference for helping whites. Several years ago I also obtained data which conformed to this pattern.

Between 1966 and 1968, my research associates and I lost nearly 1000 wallets across the length and breadth of Manhattan Island. They had some money, two dollars, and the usual melange of wallet material. Also, the wallets were identified as being owned by a white or black male, in his mid or late twenties. When each wallet was picked up from the sidewalk where it had been surreptitiously placed, hidden observers recorded whether the finder was white or black. Whites showed a slight preference for returning wallets owned by whites. Blacks showed no preference for helping other blacks.[31]

We Becoming They

These data have caused me much despair. It seems to me that they capture the most tragic and pernicious consequences of prejudice and discrimination: majority outgroup members are preferred to one's ingroup. It is a case of *we* becoming *they*.

Drs. Kenneth and Mamie Clark's experiments investigating the doll preferences of young children illustrate a similar pattern. Black children often preferred white dolls to black ones, which the Clarks interpreted as indicative of the children's feelings about themselves and members of their race.[32] In a study of ethnic relations in Israel, Yochanan Peres also found evidence illustrating how *we* becomes *they*.[33]

Oriental Jews share a cultural background with Israeli Arabs; European Jews do not. Yet, in comparison with European Jews, the Oriental Jews who responded to Peres's questions wanted to maintain a greater social distance between themselves and Arabs. They were less willing to marry *them,* be friends with *them,* or live in a neighborhood with *them.* Oriental Jews were also more likely to endorse statements prejudicial to Arabs. Peres comments, ". . . the Orientals feel that they must reject the remaining traces of their Middle Eastern origin to attain the status of the dominant European group." Perhaps the most startling observation is that anti-Arab sentiment was most pronounced among those Oriental Jews whose appearance and accent most resembled Arabs.

These data illustrate those sad occasions when aspects of self are disapproved of, even hated. They are the times when the Ninevite is *us.* When this occurs, it is as if *we* becomes *they.* For those who are like me in ways that I deplore there are no ties and no affection. Their *similarity* condemns them to *they* status, and their plight is not my concern. Instead, I am bound to others because they are *dissimilar* from that part of me which I dislike: *their* plight becomes my concern, and help is provided.

If you are depressed by my words and these findings, take heart. During the early 1970s the wallet dropping investigation was repeated.[34] Much had happened since the previous investigation: Martin Luther King and Robert Kennedy were murdered, the Black Panthers prominence waxed and waned, and the movement turned inward in the hope of articulating a black identity.

Eighty wallets were individually placed on the sidewalk. As before, an identity card indicated that the owner was either a white or black male in his mid or late twenties. This time blacks returned more wallets than before, and there was a slight tendency for them to return wallets to other blacks more frequently than to whites. Was this change indicative of a new black consciousness and a feeling that black is beautiful? Perhaps. Perhaps for blacks, the Ninevite no longer dwells within, and *we* is no longer *they*.

Notes

1. *New York Times*, Sunday, August 5, 1973, p. 32B.

2. S. Feshbach and N. Feshbach, "Influence of the Stimulus Object Upon Complementary and Supplementary Projection of Fear," *Journal of Abnormal and Social Psychology*, 66 (1963), 498–502.

3. Konrad Lorenz, *On Aggression* (New York: Bantam Books, Inc., 1967), p. 137.

4. From a news report broadcast on WINS, a local New York radio station.

5. Muzafer Sherif, "Superordinate Goals in the Reduction of Intergroup Conflicts," *American Journal of Sociology*, 63 (1958), 349–56.

6. George T. Hunt, *The Wars of the Iroquois* (Madison, Wisc.: University of Wisconsin Press, 1940).

7. Lorenz, *On Aggression*, p. 186.

8. R. Driscoll, K. E. Davis, and M. E. Lipetz, "Parental Interference and Romantic Love: The Romeo and Juliet Effect," *Journal of Personality and Social Psychology*, 24, no. 1 (1972), 1–10.

9. William Graham Sumner, *Folkways* (New York: Ginn, 1906), p. 219.

10. For two excellent and thorough reviews of this process see Morton Deutsch, *The Resolution of Conflict* (New Haven: Yale University Press, 1973) and Robert LeVine and Donald Campbell, *Ethnocentrism* (New York: John Wiley & Sons, Inc., 1972).

11. Gordon W. Allport, *The Nature of Prejudice* (New York: Doubleday & Co., Inc., Anchor Press, 1958), p. 41.

12. Lorenz, *On Aggression*, p. 182.

13. John Nance, *The Gentle Tasaday: A Stone Age People in the Philippine Rain Forest* (New York: Harcourt Brace Jovanovich, Inc., 1975).

14. Harvey Allen, "Bystander Intervention and Helping on the Subway," in Leonard Bickman and Thomas Henchy, eds., *Beyond the Laboratory: Field Research in Social Psychology* (New York: McGraw Hill Book Company, 1972).

15. Irven DeVore and K. R. L. Hall, "Baboon Ecology," in Irven DeVore, ed., *Primate Behavior* (New York: Holt, Rinehart & Winston, Inc., 1965).

16. Ervin A. Staub, "A Child in Distress: The Effects of Focussing Responsibility on Children on Their Attempts to Help," *Developmental Psychology*, 2 (1970), 152–53. A larger portion of Staub's work and thought can be found in Ervin A. Staub, "Instigation to Goodness: The Role of Social Norms and Interpersonal Influence," *Journal of Social Issues*, 28, no. 3 (1972), 131–50.

17. Harvey A. Tilker, "Socially Responsible Behavior as a Function of Observer Responsibility and Victim Feedback," *Journal of Personality and Social Psychology*, 14, no. 2 (1970), 95–100.

18. Statistical analysis suggests that the difference in the number of responses between this situation and all the rest was so great that there is very little possibility that it could have arisen by chance.

19. Tilker, "Socially Responsible," p. 100.

20. Similar conclusions are reached by Bibb Latané and John M. Darley, *The Unresponsive Bystander: Why Doesn't He Help?* (New York: Appelton-Century-Crofts, 1970).

21. For an analysis of the effects of demands for aid see L. Berkowitz, "Reactance and the Unwillingness to Help Others," *Psychological Bulletin*, 79, no. 2 (1975), 310–18.

22. Lorenz, "Behavioral Analogies to Morality," chapter seven in *On Aggression*.

23. E. Midlarsky, "Aiding Under Stress: The Effects of Competence, Dependence, Visibility, and Fatalism," *Journal of Personality and Social Psychology*, 39, no. 1 (1971), 132–49.

24. These are summarized by D. L. Krebs in his article "Altruism—An Examination of the Concept and a Review of the Literature," *Psychological Bulletin*, 73, no. 4 (1970), 258–302. Page 278 contains the synopsis of these studies.

25. Latané and Darley, *The Unresponsive Bystander*.

26. J. H. Bryan and Mary Ann Test, "Models and Helping: Naturalistic Studies in Aiding Behavior," *Journal of Personality and Social Psychology*, 6, no. 4 (1967), 400–7.

27. S. Gaertner and L. Bickman, "Effects of Race on the Elicitation of

Helping Behavior: The Wrong Number Technique," *Journal of Personality and Social Psychology*, 20, no. 2 (1971), 218–22.

28. I. M. Piliavin, J. Rodin, and J. A. Piliavin, "Good Samaritanism: An Underground Phenomenon?" *Journal of Personality and Social Psychology*, 13, no. 4 (1969), 289–99.

29. L. G. Wispe and H. B. Freshley, "Race, Sex, and Sympathetic Helping Behavior: The Broken Bag Caper," *Journal of Personality and Social Psychology*, 17, no. 1 (1971), 59–65.

30. Wispé and Freshly divide this group into two, one group consisting of those who simply pass by, and the other consisting of those who take notice of the mishap but provide no help. I find the division artificial and have combined the two for this presentation.

31. H. A. Hornstein, "Promotive Tension: The Basis of Prosocial Behavior from a Lewinian Perspective," *Journal of Social Issues*, 28, no. 3 (1972), 191–218.

32. Kenneth E. Clark and Mamie P. Clark, "Racial Identification and Preference in Negro Children," in Elizabeth E. Maccoby, Theodore M. Newcomb, Eugene L. Hartley, eds., *Readings in Social Psychology*, 3rd ed. (New York: Holt, Rinehart & Winston, Inc., 1958).

33. Y. Peres, "Ethnic Relations in Israel," *American Journal of Sociology*, 76 (1971), 1021–47.

34. H. A. Hornstein, unpublished data, Teachers College, Columbia University. Also see S. Thayer, "Lend Me Your Ears: Racial and Sexual Factors in Helping the Deaf," *Journal of Personality and Social Psychology*, 28, no. 1 (1973), 8–11. This research, conducted between November and December, 1971, in New York City, also failed to obtain any evidence of black self-discrimination.

3

Early childhood influences:

into the minds of babes

Human babies are soft, cuddly, and entirely helpless. Somebody must take care of them; otherwise, they die. Who that somebody is may vary from culture to culture, but everywhere provisions exist to solve the problem of child care. Every human baby has encounters with caretakers.

Amidst the comfort, and care, and pain of these archetypal social contacts human beings form their first social attachments. It is a monumental event. For the first time, self is experienced in relation to others, and others are experienced in relation to self. Before that point is reached the world is an egocentric blur in which objects, animate and inanimate, are experienced by infants as if they were their own appendages. At this critical juncture, however, *you* and *I* begin their emergence as psychologically distinct entities.

Mothers and fathers start to be comprehended as independent and autonomous, as discrete agencies separate from self. Yet, simultaneously, without any contradiction, children experience a special attachment to their parents which psychologically joins them in a primary and prototypic *we*. Events which affect the development and quality of this first *we* are a potentially profound determinant of a persons social orientation and future readiness to form bonds of *we* or barriers of *they*.

The First We

Psychoanalytic theorists have always been concerned with the relationship between one's sense of social relatedness and early childhood experiences with parents and other caretakers. More than three decades ago, Karen Horney discussed the effects of these experiences on the development of a person's tendency to move toward, against, or away from other people. More recently, Erik Erikson, with his customary eloquence, identified similar experiences as the origin of a person's basic trust in self and others.[1] And in 1973, in a psychoanalytic study of the roots of human aggression, Erich Fromm related early childhood experiences to the development of two types of people who have rather extreme social orientations.[2] He called them *biophils* and *necrophils*. The biophilous people, said Fromm, love life and "all that is alive." They wish to "further growth, whether in a person, a plant, an idea, or a social group." A biophil "is capable of wondering. . . loves the adventure of living. . . wants to mold and to influence by love, reason, and example."[3] Necrophilous people are frighteningly different. They are possessed by a "passionate attraction to all that is dead, decayed, putrid, sickly; it is a passion to transform that which is alive into something unalive; to destroy for the sake of destruction; the exclusive interest in all that is purely mechanical. It is a 'passion to tear apart living structures.' "[4]

Altruism, benevolence, and concern for the welfare of others are not traits that we ordinarily associate with necrophilous people. To illustrate my point: Adolf Hitler was necrophilous. His childhood provides case material which Fromm uses to support hypotheses about the way the roots of necrophilia are nurtured by early social attachments. For Fromm, nestled at the core of the disorder, like a worm in the core of an apple, is a malignantly incestuous fixation with mother. One principal progenitor of this perverse attachment is an infantile experience that is *autistic* or *nearly autistic,* which means an infant behavior pattern hallmarked by an extraordinary isolation and distance from others and a total unresponsiveness to physical or social contact. "These children never break out of the shell of their narcissism: they never experience the mother as a love object; they never form any *affective attachment* to others [italics added] but, rather, look through them as if they were inanimate objects, and they often show a particular interest in mechanical things."[5]

When the mother's character is such that extreme dependency is fostered and a child is not stimulated to crash from the emotionless grip of autistic stillness in which he is encased, then a perverse attachment to mother develops. "He is drawn to her as iron is drawn to a magnet; she is the ocean in which he wants to drown, the ground in which he wants to be buried. . . . if there is no way of being related to mother or her substitute by warm, enjoyable bonds, the relatedness to her and to the whole world must become one of final union in death."[6] Altruism, benevolence, and humane concern are clearly *not* the lot of necrophilous characters. The pernicious legacy of their morbid, early social attachments is to end life, not further it. Fortunately, the combination of events necessary to produce this outcome is not commonplace. But the dynamic relationship between early social attachments and future social orientation, upon which Fromm's thesis rests, is an inescapable fact of human life. Freud acknowledged this when he argued that the quality of relations with caretakers during infancy and childhood always has enduring effects on the development of moral motives and one's understanding (*verstehen*) of others.[7]

Empirically, the impact of early childhood experience on social orientation is most easily observed in two grossly aberrant social circumstances: the prolonged separation of an infant from his or her parents and the placement of an infant in institutional settings which are bereft of a consistent caretaker. Fromm's analysis was concerned with people whose social life was maladaptive because of childhood experience of extreme overdependency. Children who are separated from their parents or institutionalized sometimes suffer a similar fate for an opposite reason: as youngsters, they lack an opportunity to form stable, affectionate dependency ties with an adult. Paradoxically, the two extremes produce similar, but not identical fates. As you read on, pay heed to the way in which children in these circumstances also divest themselves of any interest in establishing ties with human beings.

Prolonged separation from caretakers with whom infants are attached can have ugly consequences. Their behavior and emotion bear sad testimony to the importance of the *first we* and the manner in which its development can alter social orientation and impair a person's future readiness to form social bonds. Dr. John Bowlby, a noted psychoanalyst and a foremost authority on social attachment and separation in early childhood, has identified three successive phases in the responses of children who are separated from their mothers.[8]

The beginning phase is called the *protest*. Distressed by the loss, children vent their rage by crying and tossing their small bodies to and fro, all the while pitifully searching after any cue which might suggest that their missing mothers are returning. After a time, their rage expended, these lonely, frightened children grow quiet and enter into the second phase, *despair*. With occasional whimpers, they mounfully withdraw, shirking any social contact. But this too passes, and when the withdrawal ends all about may applaud what they believe to be a successful conclusion to a sad event. How wrong they are!

The renewed social contact is hollow. It is part of the third and final phase, *detachment*, which is characterized by a morbid lack of concern about social attachments. Increasingly self-centered, the children's only intense concern outside of self is with material possessions. Things replace people as the central objects of their emotional lives. It is as if feelings were no longer invested in people because their departures have proven too unpredictable and painful. The capacity that these children once had for forming social bonds, for experiencing the feeling "you and I are *we* ," has been tragically impaired.

A similar impairment has been observed in orphaned children who, for lack of a consistent caretaker, never had the opportunity to form social attachments. Relevant data are available in several studies of orphans whose ages ranged from three and one-half to twelve years.[9] For the first three years of their lives some of these children lived in an institution where no one person cared for them all of the time. On or about their third birthday all this was changed when they moved to a foster home. But by then it was too late. The harm was done. When they were compared with other orphans who had always lived in a foster home, vast differences between the groups emerged. Even after living in a foster home for several years, children who were institutionalized for their first three years of life exhibited considerably more abnormal and deviant social behavior. They lied, stole, destroyed property, and hit other children far more than their counterparts who spent their entire infancy in foster homes. Most importantly, the children who were initially institutionalized were incapable of developing warm emotional ties. Their interpersonal relationships tended to be superficial and without any emotional involvement. In interaction they were cold, distant, and cautious. Like the children studied by Drs. Bowlby and Fromm, as infants these children suffered a devastating disruption of the opportunity to form close, warm social attachments, and the result was an impaired readiness to form social bonds.

Devastatingly dramatic events like being separated from one's parents or orphaned are not the only ones that adversely alter a person's readiness to form social bonds and say "You and I are *we*." Nor is the development of positive social attachments guaranteed by the continued presence of parents or parental surrogates. Caretakers differ greatly in the relationships that they build with children. Quietly, slowly, these relationships shape that part of personality which involves social orientation and the readiness to form bonds of *we* or barriers of *they*. The *I* that is available to relate to *you* in order to produce *we* is very much determined by parental child-rearing practices. Some parents create childhood experiences within which the developing person becomes open and responsive to building bonds of *we;* others create experiences which impair their children's readiness to form bonds of *we* or predispose them toward creating barriers of *they*.

The I *in* We

For one moment join me in the simplified, but potentially fruitful, assumption that every human being can be placed somewhere on a continuum that ranges from socially inclusive to socially exclusive. Each of us know people who act if there were no strangers. Everyone is a potential friend, a *we*. Their actual or anticipated contacts with other humans are predominated by a sense of belonging and feelings of being included. They tend to be optimistic about people's concerns for one another's welfare, and in social encounters they are predisposed to identify a basis for commonality. Differences tend to be minimized. Behaviorally, they are gregarious, affable, open, warm, and accepting. These people have a heightened readiness to form *we*-group ties.

By contrast, there is another group of people with whom we have each had experiences in whom feelings of isolation and social distance predominate. They are cynical and pessimistic about people's concerns for one another's welfare. In social encounters there is no searching for commonality. Differences become objects of central concern. Behaviorally, they withdraw from social contact, maintain strong prejudices, and assume a cold, aloof, if not unfriendly posture. In these people the readiness to form *we*-group ties is constricted to a narrow range of people. One group with this social orientation and behavior pattern has been labeled *authoritarian.* Their childhood experiences have been the subject of extensive research.

Discipline, rules, and obligations are the very essence of the relationship between nascent authoritarians and their parents. Harsh and unloving, their parents demand obedience and dispense severe punishment for what they identify as undesirable behavior. To observers the punishment seems arbitrary and the rules rigid. Punishment is unaccompanied by explanations since the parents regard their status and authority as clear and unquestionable.

Angry, perhaps filled with hate, the child is too overwhelmed by fear to act on these negative feelings, which are upsetting, dangerous, and confusing. They must be expelled from consciousness. In their place emerges a denial consisting of safer emotions and thoughts in which parents, parental surrogates, and all authority are idealized. Hostile feelings are displaced away from authorities who are envisioned to be omnipotent and strong onto subordinate and weak outgroups. Disapproved of thoughts and impulses which portend punishment if expressed, are projected onto the outgroups as well, and *they* become the contemptible custodians of the "evil" that is denied in oneself.[10]

Like Fromm's necrophilous character and Bowlby's *detached* children, authoritarians tend toward an interest in what is mechanical and objective, rather than human or emotional.[11] They emerge from childhood as misanthropes, dominated by cynical beliefs about people.[12] Their social orientation is plainly evident in the beliefs to which they subscribe: "People can be divided into two distinct classes, the weak and the strong," "Familiarity breeds contempt"; "Novels or stories which contain mainly action, romance, and adventure are more interesting than those that tell about what people think and feel"; "When you come right down to it, it's human nature never to do anything without an eye to one's own profit."[13]

Compared to their egalitarian counterparts, authoritarians' behavior toward others, including complete strangers, tends to be more untrusting, untrustworthy, and competitive.[14] In all likelihood this "antisocial" behavior is influenced by distorting fears and hostility which stimulate a conviction that others agree with their views about human nature and social relationships. Therefore, when they treat others as *they* by behaving competitively and intolerantly, they are doing so in the fond delusion that their behavior is fully justified: they are simply doing unto others before the others do unto them.

One hundred and thirty-nine Purdue University students further illustrated the consequences of this childhood experience on social orientation by demonstrating the restricted conditions under which authoritarians show mercy toward other human beings.[15] Pretending to be part of a jury, each of these students read a case allegedly from the files of the Dean of Men at the University of Toledo. The defendant was a junior attending the College of Arts and Sciences. His name was William Davidson.

William was charged with theft of an examination for a course in which he was enrolled. To the charges William answered, "Dr. Howell sent me to the duplicating room to pick up a copy of an article for a course I was in. When I got there, no one was around, so I went in to find the article myself. While I was looking for the article, I found a copy of the test I was going to take the next day. I had been studying for that test for a week, and I was really worried about it. I just impulsively picked up the test and walked out with it." How great is William's guilt? How severe should be his punishment?

In order to help these student-jurors in their judgment of William some biographical data were provided. They were deliberately constructed to lead the student-jurors to believe that either William completely agreed with their attitudes on five issues, or he completely disagreed with them. About the student-jurors one other bit of information was obtained: their tendency toward authoritarianism. (The word *tendency* in the preceding sentence is critical. These students' scores were generally within the normal range, not in the extremes. Therefore, the findings are applicable to you and me, people who tend to be more or less authoritarian.)

Authoritarians discriminated between similar and dissimilar Williams more than their egalitarian counterparts. When asked, "How positively or negatively do you feel about the defendant?" egalitarians liked the similar William and the dissimilar one almost equally. But with authoritarians that was not the case. Those who encountered a William who was similar to them liked him well enough, but those who encountered a dissimilar William did not care for him at all. The same pattern of results emerged when judgments of guilt and punishment were considered. Compared to egalitarians, authoritarians were far more likely to judge a dissimilar William, a *they*, as guilty and punish him severely. The legacy of their upbringing was overwhelmingly evident. For authoritarians, the boundaries of *we* and *they*, ingroup and outgroup, were intolerantly and narrowly drawn. Mindful of every difference, they unsympathetically decided, "mercy is for *us*, but not for *them*."

This same pattern of ingroup favoritism and outgroup prejudice was evident in a related investigation conducted by a psychologist named Gaertner.[16] His study and my interpretation of it both rest upon a firm foundation of earlier research which demonstrated that more authoritarian dispositions and antiblack sentiments[17] are found in people at the conservative, rather than liberal, end of the political spectrum. (It does not follow that conservatives are authoritarian but liberals are not. Once again I am talking about relative scores on a personality test that fall within the normal range. I am not talking about extreme character patterns.)

Subjects in Dr. Gaertner's study were members of either the Liberal or Conservative parties of New York City. They were home when the telephone rang and a voice, which was either heavy with New York intonations or flowing with a southern black dialect, asked for Ralph's Garage. Since the caller quickly learned that he had not reached Ralph's he explained that he was stranded on a highway and now had no more dimes for telephone calls. He asked, "Could you please telephone the garage for me?" Liberal party members were more egalitarian. They were equally likely to help white and black callers. Conservative party members, like the more authoritarian Purdue students, discriminated. They were much more likely to help a white victim than a black one (92 percent *vs.* 64 percent) and they helped a greater percentage of whites than did Liberal party members (92 percent *vs.* 76 percent). The author concludes: "It seems that Conservatives have greater social responsibility toward others of their *own kind* than Liberals. (italics added) The Liberal's sense of morality may require him to help others regardless of his personal feelings toward the victim." I believe that Dr. Gaertner's observations reflect the tendency of Conservatives toward authoritarianism and the accompnaying disposition to respond intolerantly to indicators of personal difference by drawing sharp boundaries between *we* and *they*.

Authoritarians are socially exclusive. Their prematurely definitive and harshly judgmental distinctions between ingroups and outgroups are fruitless attempts to resolve their own intrapsychic conflict. Their prejudice is an almost indelible aftermath of the quality of their childhood attachments to principal caretakers. The psychological processes involved, and their consequences, are eloquently captured by the late Gordon Allport in his classic work, *The Nature of Prejudice*,[18] which concerns not only authoritarians but all people who are prejudiced and intolerant. He writes:

> Some modern theories of love and hate. . . . maintain that the original orientation of all men is toward a trusting and affiliative philosophy of life. This disposition grows naturally out of the early dependent relationship of mother and child, of earth and creature. Affiliation is the source of all happiness. When hatred and animosity grow in a life, they are crippling distortions of this naturally affiliative trend. Hate results from the mishandling of frustration and deprivations that have been allowed to disintegrate the very core of ego. If this view is correct, the development of mature democratic personalities is largely a matter of building inner security. Only when life is free from intolerable threats, or when these threats are adequately handled with inner strength, can one be at ease with all sorts and conditions of men.[19]

Intolerant, prejudiced, authoritarian people are not at ease. The baggage of their youth is filled with inescapable hates and fears. Mistrusting their own impulses, they are wary of others and the impulses that they might possess. Their world becomes a jungle which must be carefully scrutinized because it is filled with human beings who harbor the "evil" that they painfully learned to deny in themselves. Socially inclusive people are different. Like the more egalitarian Purdue students and Liberal party members in New York City, they are more at ease with "all sorts and conditions of men." Mercy, help, and humane concern are given freely with less regard to cues that others may use as signals for dividing the world into *we* and *they*. It is not that they are less able to see the cues. Proclivity, not perceptive ability, has been altered by their childhood experience.

Socially inclusive people are tolerant of differences. For that reason, bonds of *we* are more prevalent in their lives than barriers of *they*. A steady stream of evidence has tied personality traits associated with this social orientation to selfless behavior. Helping and altruism have been empirically related to social extroversion, affiliative tendencies (gregariousness), sociability, and attractiveness as a friend.[20] After reviewing the available evidence on the relationship between personality traits and altruism, Professor Dennis Krebs says,

> . . . altruistic children seem to be better adjusted socially than others—they are less aggressive, quarrelsome, and competitive, and they are more emotionally stable. . . . . College-age female altruists are socially oriented—they are clyclothymic [*author's note:* socially extroverted] and have social (versus political or economic) values. They are nurturant people with low needs for achievement or dominance. College-age male altruists also tend to be socially oriented; they are free from neuroticism, and tend to think that they control their fates.[21]

These personality traits, which belong at the socially inclusive end of our serviceable, but very hypothetical, continuum, are born and nurtured in a childhood that is a world apart from the one experienced by children from the socially exclusive end of the continuum. It is a world that tends to be filled with the kind of parental warmth and nurturance that stimulates affectionate social bonds between parent and child.[22] In this setting children do not develop morbid fears about their own impulses and there is no need to project them onto outgroups. Their social world is no jungle. It is a comparatively safe and secure place, where a readiness to form bonds of *we* prevails over any inclination to form barriers of *they*.

Most of us escape the extreme consequences manifest in authoritarian personalities, but very few human beings grow up free of any disposition to evaluatively judge *we* and *they*. It is an unintended byproduct of human socialization. In the course of development, the self incorporates attributes to which it is exposed. Families, tribes, neighborhoods, ethnic groups, and other surrounding social entities are the inevitable sources of influence simply because they are there.

Robert Louis Stevenson once wrote,

> *Little Indian, Sioux or Crow*
> *Little frosty Eskimo*
> *Little Turk or Japanee*
> *Oh! don't you wish that you were me?*
>
> *You have seen the scarlet trees*
> *And the lions over seas,*

You have eaten ostrich eggs
And turned the turtles off their legs.

Such a life is very fine,
But it's not so nice as mine:
You must often, as you trod
Have wearied not *to be abroad.*

You have curious things to eat,
I am fed on proper meat;
You must dwell beyond the foam,
But I am safe and live at home.
    Little Indian, Sioux or Crow,
    Little frosty Eskimo
    Little Turk or Japanee
Oh! don't you wish that you were me?[23]

The habits, patterns, and beliefs of our community become part of us, and *I* emerges, new, unique, and yet inevitably lockstitched into the fabric of our fellows. *We* and *they* become important social categories because they are symbolically related to our self-identity and our earliest and most profound emotional ties.

Identification and Models: We Do as We Do

Socially inclusive people are aroused by another's plight not only because their social orientations were molded through the experience of warm, nurturant childhood attachments, but also because they once had opportunities to observe loved and loving caretakers being concerned about the welfare of other human beings.

What they learn from parental behavior and the activities of other adult caretakers is not critical simply because it informs children about how they should behave when faced with an opportunity to donate to this or that specific charity; nor is it critical simply because they learn, by example, to share their resources or to lift the fallen in this or that specific situation. Behavior of adult caretakers is critical because it has impact which goes beyond the specific concrete situation in which an observation occurs. For that reason, adult behavior carries the potential to shape a youngster's social orientation and sense of social relatedness. It carries an implicit message about others, and one's relationship and responsibility toward them. What emerges from repeated observations of adult behavior in various situations is not a catalog of carefully indexed and cross-referenced behavioral examples of what to do and not to do on each of those specific occasions, but a style of relating to the social world.[24] Investigations of the childhood origins of motivation to participate in civil rights activity and to rescue Jews from the Nazi holocaust provide pertinent evidence.

Professor David Rosenhan of Stanford University conducted the investigation of civil rights workers.[25] Forty-six black and white men and women were involved in the part of Professor Rosenhan's study with which I will be concerned. He divided these people into two groups, and labeled them the *partially committed* and the *fully committed*. "The first had been involved in civil rights only to the extent of having participated in one or two freedom rides. The second had been continuously active for at least a year, commonly longer, mainly in the south with such diverse projects as voter registration and education of the underprivileged."[26]

Depth interviews with members of these two groups revealed that principal differences between them ". . . concerned the affective relationship to the socializing agents during the respondents' formative years, and. . . the kind of socializers to which they were exposed."[27] The fully committed reported a relationship with their parents that was akin to the one that we have now identified as being characteristic of socially inclusive people. It was warm and positive, with mutual respect between parents and children. Even when disagreements existed, Professor Rosenhan comments, ". . . one easily sensed considerable fondness between parents and child. Even when there was serious cause for disagreement, they seemed to be able to tolerate and respect each other's view."[28]

Relationships between the partially committed and their parents were reminiscent of those that we have associated with socially exclusive people. They were described in "negative" or "ambivalent" terms. "Many described their relations with the socializing parent as downright hostile during their formative years and at best, cool and avoidant during the time they were interviewed."[29] Professor Rosenhan reports detecting discomfort, anxiety, hostility, and guilt between child and parent, and possibly parent and child. Some of the partially committed had been brutalized and in several instances they had run away from home.

Against this background of difference between the partially and fully committed, Professor Rosenhan discovered something additional. During the fully committed's formative years they had had the opportunity to observe one or both their parents dedicatedly engaged in some altruistic cause. Unlike the parents of partially committed, who preached about social and moral concerns but acted otherwise, the parents of fully committed displayed a consistent, unambivalent concern for the welfare of other human beings. (Professor Rosenhan notes that the parents of a third group, whose only civil rights activity was to make financial contributions, were neither consistently nor even hypocritically altruistic. Altruism was simply not reported as being part of their lives.)

Years later, when Rosenhan's partially and fully committed interviewees reached their maturity, the issues had changed—Saco and Vanzetti were dead and the Spanish Civil war was ended—but the messages contained in the altruistic behavior of some parents were recreated in the activities of their children. Like their parents before them, the fully committed could not respond to the plight of their fellows with apathy or token gestures. Others were in need and they helped.

Just about the time that many of the fully committed civil rights workers were learning to walk or entering elementary schools, a savage slaughter of millions of Jewish men, women and children was beginning. It was a time of barbarism and bravery. Amidst the human decadence there was a small group of people who could not stand by idly. They gallantly risked their lives in an effort to rescue Jews.

In-depth interviews of twenty-seven "rescuers" are reported in an article by Dr. Perry London.[30] After considering the data, he identified three traits which were shared by many of the twenty-seven: rescuers had a *spirit of adventurousness;* they had a *sense of being socially marginal* and perhaps for that reason experienced a sense of symbolic similarity to the Jews that they were rescuing, who also stood on society's periphery; and, rescuers had an *intense identification with a parental model of moral conduct.* If the sins of fathers (and mothers) are visited upon their children, then so are their good deeds. The fully committed civil rights workers and the rescuers of Jews from Nazi barbarism had no need to ask "for whom the bell tolls!" Decades before the question was answered by the deeds of their parents: when it tolls, it tolls for us all.

Development of Empathy: The You in Me

Fiction is often rewarding because we share the joys and sorrows of heroes and heroines. For just a few moments the boundaries between self and others are transcended as their experiences are apprehended. The same occurs in the course of a day's activities when loved ones, friends, colleagues, and even strangers provide the stimuli for similar experiences. Psychologists and laymen use the same word to describe this phenomenon. It is called *empathy*.

In the *International Encyclopedia of the Social Sciences*, Professor Lauren G. Wispé briefly defines empathy as, "the self-conscious awareness of the consciousness of others." He says that it is a "self-conscious effort to share and accurately comprehend the presumed consciousness of another person, including his thoughts, feelings, perceptions, and muscular tensions, as well as their causes."[31] Empathy is a psychological reaching out, a way of including another's experience in your own. It is the representation of *you* in *me*, and it is potentially capable of producing feelings of *we*.

Of course, as one investigator of empathic processes has said, "Our sharing of the feelings of another does not. . . *necessarily* imply that we will act or even feel impelled to act in a supportive way when we are reacting to another's sorrows. We might avoid the other person because he makes us feel bad. . . ." "Nevertheless," he goes on to say, "a person may be moved by another's pain to help the other, or to help another attain and sustain a happy experience."[32]

The truth of these remarks was made painfully clear to me on one occasion when I was employed to mediate in a social conflict. I asked members of two feuding groups to briefly reverse roles in order to induce an empathic understanding in each of them of the other's point of view.[33] Although all the people involved were members of the same organization, they were committed to rather opposite sociopolitical philosophies. After reversing roles, the conflict was not eased, nor was a basis for collaboration established. In fact, the complete absence of *we*-group ties was manifest in a single comment. One fellow said, "Before I pretended that I was them, I only thought that they were bastards; now I *know* that they are." When basic values are in conflict, empathic insight, knowledge produced by the *you* in *me*, does not produce positive social bonds. These bonds are produced only when knowledge made available by a study of the *you* in *me*, reveals unconflicting similarities of interests, values, or experience.[34]

Two centuries ago Adam Smith related the human capacity for unselfish behavior to empathy when he said, "How selfish so ever man may be supposed, There are evidently some principles in his nature which interest him in the fortune of others and render their happiness necessary to him, though he derives nothing from it. . . ." Adam Smith speculated that this occurs because human beings are capable of ". . . changing places in fancy with the sufferer, that we come either to conceive or to be affected by what he feels."[35]

Two centuries after Adam Smith wrote these words, in two separate investigations[36] adults were induced to "change places in fancy with a sufferer, so as to conceive or be affected by what he felt." They helped more than their counterparts who were not induced to be empathic. But people are not equal in their capacity or disposition to be "aware of the consciousness of others."

Young children are too egocentric to be able to "change places in fancy." Accurate role-taking is a capacity that develops with age and cognitive capacities.[37] Consequently, young children might be expected to lack insight into the plight of sufferers. It is very likely that this inability exists and contributes greatly to one rather consistent research finding: until preadolescence, generosity and other forms of altruistic behavior increase with age.[38]

Authoritarians also lack empathic capacity.[39] Even after extensive conversation with another person they are less able to identify with the other's attitudes than more egalitarian people. Given what we have learned about authoritarians and what we know about the development of empathy this should come as no surprise.

Some of the most enlightening material on the development of empathy is contained in a creative series of investigations conducted by University of Pennsylvania psychologist, Justin Aronfreed. His investigations are related to a common observation: children frequently offer their playthings and soggy bits of food to adult bystanders.[40] Adults, especially parents, often delight in these offerings and respond with joyous squeals, increased attention, and overt physical affection. Children, in turn, delight in these responses to what I shall call their *prototypic* generosity. Empathic responsiveness is born when their feelings of delight and pleasure become "attached" to the adults' gestures and squeals which were elicited by their prototypic generosity. If on subsequent occasions the proper situational cues are present, the generous behavior is once again emitted. Why? Because children act on the basis of anticipated outcomes. They learn to produce behavior in others which is empathically pleasant, and to terminate behavior which is empathically distressing.

In one of his investigations, Professor Aronfreed began by having some children observe and experience an unusual event.[41] A young woman responded to a very ordinary red light by shouting, " *There's the light*," grinning broadly and hugging the child. Other children sat with more dispassionate (no broad grins) and/or unaffectionate (no hugs) women. After several repetitions of this episode, each child was faced with a minor dilemma. They could pull one of two levers. One produced M & M candies for them; the other produced the red light, which was so mysteriously stimulating for the lady. Joyous, hugging women were more likely to be "helped" by a sacrifice of delectable M & M's, than dispassionate, unaffectionate women.

Professor Aronfreed's experiment may be thought of as a small scale analogy to human socialization. If this viewpoint is correct, then it is reasonable to conclude that the development of empathically altruistic dispositions is very much contingent on the quality of parental behavior. Parents who shower their children with rewarding hugs, touches, squeals, kisses, and hugs after acts of prototypic generosity are more likely to rear empathic, altruistic children than those who are more cooly dispassionate about such benevolent gestures. This interpretation of Professor Aronfreed's work underscores the importance of the quality of parental behavior, which is consistent with this chapter's point of view. There is an equally plausible interpretation, however, which is consistent with this book's entire theme. It argues that these children were doing nothing more than showing a predisposition to help someone who was liked because she was so rewarding.[42] One might say that the bonds of *we* were solidified by her unusual display of affection, and the children were relatively more disposed toward helping someone to whom they were tied through the bonds of *we*.

Parental behavior can also be identified as the cause of empathy and altruistic behavior in an investigation of children's considerateness of other children.[43] The investigation compared three groups of children whose parents either (1) punished their children for transgressions; (2) arbitrarily defined right and wrong for them with no additional explanations; or (3) explained moral conduct in terms of the consequences that their behavior had for the welfare of others. As nearly every investigation of this issue has demonstrated, punishment and authoritative edicts which prescribe duties and responsibilities are both to little avail. Children in the third group, the ones whose parents used reasoning that caused them to attend to the consequences of their behavior on others, were the most considerate. Unlike the other two groups of parents, theirs stimulated an empathic response. Because of their parents' intervention, the experiences of other people were transplanted into their world. *You* was present in *me*, and the knowledge that that made available provided an empathic basis for regulating behavior.

Empathic attentiveness to the experiences of others and understanding of one's responsibility for others' welfare are also subtly shaped as a child conducts him or herself in accordance with implicit or explicit family rules. A study completed at Harvard University contains pertinent evidence:[44] Children who lived in cultures in which they had prescribed responsibility for the family's welfare were more likely to be helpful to others than children from cultures where fewer or more trivial responsibilities were theirs. Perhaps we can conclude: responsibility for *thee* stimulates awareness of the *you* in *me*.

Dr. Ervin Staub illustrated this effect when he had a number of children teach other children about various subjects.[45] As teachers, they had the experience of responsibility for another. Attentiveness to their "students'" needs was elicited by the very nature of their role. If they were to be good teachers, they were compelled to experience *you* in *me*. Subsequently, these youngsters and another group who lacked the experience of being "teachers" were both given an opportunity to write letters to hospitalized children. Ex-teachers wrote an average of 1.5 letters. The other youngsters wrote an average of less than one letter each. They did not have a heightened sense of themselves as people who are attentive to and responsible for others' welfare.

Similar consequences occur because of childhood experiences that arise as a by-product of at least two conditions of family structure. In ordinary financial circumstances, children from large families have a greater number of opportunities for relating to and caring for siblings than children from small families. Because they have so many added experiences with assuming responsibility, we might guess that they would be more disposed to help others in need. It is a good guess. Several investigations demonstrate that children from large families are more generous, helpful, and altruistic than children from small families.[46]

Like children from large families and those who are directed by parents or the surrounding culture to attend to others' welfare, older siblings also have a comparatively larger number of opportunities for experiencing *you* in *me*. Their behavior reflects the trend that we have been observing: they are more likely to help others than their younger brothers and sisters.[47]

Readiness to experience bonds of *we* or barriers of *they* is not biologically determined, nor is it constant as our lives move across time and space. It is nurtured in the course of our upbringing by the quality of our relations with parents which affects the *I* in *we*, by observations of parental behavior which affect knowledge of what *we* do, and by experiences that heighten and reward empathy, an awareness of the *you* in *me*.

Readiness to form bonds of *we* or barriers of *they* is not fixed at birth. It reflects the vagaries of childhood experience and social circumstance. That is evolution's unique and double-edged bequest to humankind. In the fundamental human malleability that this fact implies lies the essence of our species' hope and dilemma.

Notes

1. Karen Horney, *Neurotic Personality of Our Times* (New York: W. W. Norton & Company, Inc., 1937); *Self-analysis* (New York: W. W. Norton & Company, Inc., 1942); *Our Inner Conflicts* (New York: W. W. Norton & Company, Inc., 1945); Erik H. Erikson, *Childhood and Society* (New York: W. W. Norton & Company, Inc., 1950); *Identity: Youth and Crisis* (New York: W. W. Norton & Company, Inc., 1968).

2. Erich Fromm, *The Anatomy of Human Destructiveness* (New York: Holt, Rinehart & Winston, Inc., 1973).

3. Fromm, Ibid, p. 365.

4. Fromm, Ibid, p. 332.

5. Fromm, Ibid, p. 362.

6. Fromm, Ibid, p. 363.

7. Sigmund Freud, *The Origins of Psychoanalysis: Lectures to Wilhelm Flies, Drafts and Notes, 1887 to 1902* (New York: Basic Books, Inc., Publishers, 1954).

8. John Bowlby, *Attachment and Loss, Volume I: Attachment* (New York: Basic Books, Inc., Publishers, 1969).

9. W. Goldfarb, "Infant Rearing and Problem Behavior," *American Journal of Orthopsychiatry,* 13 (1943), 249–66; Goldfarb, "The Effects of Early Institutional Care on Adolescent Personality," *Journal of Experimental Education,* 12 (1943), 107–29; Goldfarb, "The Effects of Early Institutional Care on Adolescent Personality" (graphic Rorschach data), *Child Development,* 14 (1943), 213–25; Goldfarb, "The Effects of Early Institutional Care on Adolescent Personality" (Rorschach data), *American Journal of Orthopsychiatry,* 14 (1944), 441–47; Goldfarb, "Psychological Privation in Infancy and Subsequent Adjustment,"*American Journal of Orthopsychiatry,* 15 (1945), 247–255.

10. Theodore Adorno, Egon Frankel-Brunswik, Daniel Levinson, and Robert Sanford, *The Authoritarian Personality* (New York: Harper & Row, Publishers, 1950).

11. Adorno et al., Ibid.

12. R. Christie and P. Cook, "A Guide to Published Literature relating to the Authoritarian Personality through 1956," *Journal of Psychology,* 45 (1958), 171–99; P. L. Sullivan and J. Adelson, "Ethnocentrism and Misanthropy," *Journal of Abnormal and Social Psychology,* 49 (1954), 246–50.

13. Adorno et al., *Authoritarian Personality.*

14. M. Deutsch, "Trust, Trustworthiness, and the F Scale," *Journal of Abnormal and Social Psychology,* 61 (1960), 138–40; L. S. Wrightsman, "Personality and Attitudinal Correlates of Trusting and Trustworthy Behaviors in a Two-Person Game," *Journal of Personality and Social Psychology,* 4 (1966), 328–32. For a general review see H. H. Kelley and A. J. Stahelski, "Social Interaction Basis of Cooperators' and Competitors' Beliefs About Others," *Journal of Personality and Social Psychology,* 16 (1970), 66–91.

15. H. E. Mitchell and D. Byrne, "The Defendant's Dilemma: Effects of Juror's Attitudes and Authoritarianism on Judicial Decisions," *Journal of Personality and Social Psychology,* 25 (1972), 123–29.

16. S. Gaertner, "Helping Behavior and Racial Discrimination Among Liberals and Conservatives," *Journal of Personality and Social Psychology,* 25 (1973), 335–41.

17. Adorno et al., *Authoritarian Personality;* H. McClosky, "Conservatism and Personality," *American Political Science Review,* 52 (1958), 27–45; Lloyd Free and Hadley Cantril, *The Political Beliefs of Americans: A Study of Public Opinion* (New Brunswick: Rutgers University Press, 1967).

18. Gordon W. Allport, *The Nature of Prejudice* (New York: Doubleday & Company, Inc., 1958).

19. G. W. Allport, Ibid., p. 411.

20. R. Cattell and J. Horowitz, "Objective Personality Tests Investigating the Structure of Altruism in Relation to Source Traits, A, H, and L,"

Journal of Personality and Social Psychology, 21 (1952), 103–17; R. W. Friedrichs, "Alter Versus Ego: An Exploratory Assessment of Altruism," *American Sociological Review*, 25 (1960), 496–508.

21. D. Krebs, "Altruism—An Examination of the Concept and a Review of the Literature," *Psychological Bulletin*, 73 (1970), 258–302.

22. A. L. Baldwin, "The Effect of Home Environment on Nursery School Behavior," *Child Development*, 20 (1949), 49–62; A. L. Baldwin, J. Kalhorn, and F. H. Breese, "The Appraisal of Present Behavior," *Psychological Monographs*, 63, no. 299 (1949); D. Baumrind, "Child Care Practices Anteceding Three Patterns of Preschool Behavior," *Genetic Psychology Monograph*, 1967, 43–88.

23. Robert Louis Stevenson, "Foreign Children," *A Child's Garden of Verses* (New York: Avenel Books).

24. The assumption that children learn through observation is based upon the work of Albert Bandura, discussions of which can be found in Albert Bandura and Richard H. Walters, *Social Learning and Personality Development* (New York: Holt, Rinehart & Winston, Inc., 1963) and Albert Bandura, *Principles of Behavior Modification* (New York: Holt, Rinehart & Winston, Inc., 1969). The last chapter of the second of these books is entitled "Symbolic Control of Behavioral Change." It includes ideas which are addressed again by Bandura in his presidential address to the American Psychological Association meetings in New Orleans in August, 1974, "Behavior Theory and the Models of Man." Both of these are relevant background for ideas included in the next paragraph.

25. David Rosenhan, "The Natural Socialization of Altruistic Autonomy," in Jacqueline Macaulay and Leonard Berkowitz, eds., *Altruism and Helping Behavior* (New York: Academic Press, Inc., 1970).

26. Rosenhan, Ibid., p. 260.

27. Rosenhan, Ibid., p. 260.

28. Rosenhan, Ibid., p. 261.

29. Rosenhan, Ibid., p. 262.

30. Perry London, "The Rescuers: Motivational Hypotheses about Christians who Saved Jews from the Nazis," in Macaulay and Berkowitz, eds., *Altruism and Helping Behavior* (New York: Academic Press, Inc., 1970).

31. Lauren G. Wispé, "Sympathy and Empathy," in the *International Encyclopedia of the Social Sciences* (New York: The Macmillan Company, and the Free Press, 1968), p. 441.

32. Ezra Stotland, "Exploratory Investigations of Empathy," in L. Berkowitz, ed., *Advances in Experimental Social Psychology, Volume 4* (New York: Academic Press, Inc., 1969), p. 272.

33. This procedure is a familiar one to organizational consultants.

References to its use and related matters are Robert R. Blake, Herbert A. Shepard, and Jane S. Mouton, *Managing Intergroup Conflict in Industry* (Houston: Gulf, 1964); W. Schmidt and R. Tannenbaum, "Management of Differences," *Harvard Business Review*, 38 (November–December, 1960), 107–115; Richard Walton, *Interpersonal Peacemaking: Confrontations and Third Party Consultation* (Reading, Mass.: Addison-Wesley, 1969).

34. D. W. Johnson, "Role Reversal: A Summary and Review of Research," *International Journal of Group Tensions*, 1 (1971), 318–34.

35. Adam Smith, "The Theory of Moral Sentiments," in Herbert Schneider, ed., *Adam Smith's Moral and Political Philosophy* (New York: Hafner Publishing Co., Inc., 1948).

36. D. Aderman and L. Berkowitz, "Empathy, Outcome, and Altruism," Proceedings of the 77th Annual Convention of the American Psychological Association, 4 (1969), 379–80; Dennis L. Krebs, "Empathically Experienced Affect and Altruism" (unpublished doctoral dissertation, Harvard University, 1970).

37. P. Bowers and P. London, "Developmental Correlates of Role-playing Ability," *Child Development*, 36 (1965), 499–508; M. H. Feffer and V. Gourevitch, "Cognitive Aspects of Role Taking in Children," *Journal of Personality and Social Psychology*, 28 (1960), 383–96. I am concerned particularly with affective rather than perceptual perspective taking, although both are relevant. Information about these matters can be found in John H. Flavell, *The Development of Role-taking and Communication Skills in Children* (New York: John Wiley & Sons, Inc., 1968); R. Dymond, A. Hughes, and V. Raabe, "Measurable Changes in Empathy with Age," *Journal of Consulting Psychology*, 16 (1952), 202–6; and Johnson, "Role Reversal."

38. Summaries of this research can be found in J. H. Bryan, "Why Children Help: A Review," *Journal of Social Issues*, 28 (1972), 86–104 (especially pp. 97–99); Krebs, "Empathically Experienced" (especially pp. 288–90); and D. L. Rosenhan, "Learning Theory and Prosocial Behavior, *Journal of Social Issues*, 28 (1972), 151–163 (especially pp. 159–160).

39. Kelley and Stahleski have summarized the relevant research on pages 83–85 of their article, "Social Interaction Basis of Cooperators' and Competitors' Beliefs About Others."

40. Justin Aronfreed, chapter six in "Sympathy and Altruism," *Conduct and Conscience: The Socialization of Internalized Control Over Behavior* (New York: Academic Press, Inc., 1968).

41. Reported in Aronfreed, Ibid., pp. 143–47.

42. Krebs, "Empathically Experienced"; E. Midlarsky and J. H. Bryan, "Training Charity in Children," *Journal of Personality and Social Psychology*, 5 (1967), 408–15.

43. M. L. Hoffman, "Parent Discipline and the Child's Consideration for Others," *Child Development*, 34 (1963), 573–88; M. L. Hoffman and H. D. Saltzstein, "Parent Discipline and the Child's Moral Development," *Journal of Personality and Social Psychology*, 5 (1967), 45–57.

44. L. M. W. Whiting and B. Whiting, "The Behavior of Children in Six Cultures," reported in E. Staub, "To Rear a Prosocial Child: Reasoning, Learning by Doing, and Learning by Teaching Others," presented at the Symposium on Contemporary Issues in Moral Development, Loyola University, Chicago, December, 1973.

45. Reported in Staub, Ibid.

46. S. Ribal, "Social Character and Meanings of Selfishness and Altruism," *Sociology and Social Research*, 47 (1963), 311–21; R. Uqurel-Semin, "Moral Behavior and Moral Judgment in Children," *Journal of Abnormal and Social Psychology*, 47 (1952), 502–16.

47. E. Staub, "A Child in Distress: the Influence of Age and Number of Witnesses on Children's Attempts to Help," *Journal of Personality and Social Psychology*, 14 (1970), 130–40; E. Staub, "Helping a Person in Distress: the Influence of Implicit and Explicit 'Rules' or Conduct of Children and Adults," *Journal of Personality and Social Psychology*, 17 (1971), 137–45.

4

Human evolution:

a hunting we will go

Savannahs are open grasslands. Animals that burrow beneath the earth and those that fly above it, grass-eating mammals and the long-clawed, sharp-toothed creatures who prey upon them, have all found a suitable ecological niche on the savannah. But the soft gentleness of that green-carpeted, pristine land is in some ways deceptive. Savannah residents survive either by eating the available vegetation or each other, and the open grassland is treacherous—it provides predators and prey with few places to hide or climb. Without some unique defense, attack, or escape capacity—without speed, strength, slashing dagger-like teeth or claws—animals seem illequipped to compete for survival on savannahs. Yet, between three and four million years ago, just such an apparently ill-equipped creature journeyed onto the great savannahs of prehistoric Africa.

The creature was a small, upright primate, weighing approximately fifty or sixty pounds and standing about four feet high. It possessed no great speed, no claws, and no massive teeth for fighting. All in all, the creature, by name *Australopithicus,* was a comparative weakling, an odds-on failure at savannah living.

Australopithicus was neither bold nor foolish. In all probability its migration onto the savannahs was unwittingly prompted by a search for food. For eons before similar primates dwelled in lush forests. Some of them were aboreal, and swung through the tree tops either by using their great tails or brachiating, hand-over-hand. Others were ground-dwelling apes, like present-day gorillas. They were all primarily vegetarians who survived by foraging in the bountifulness with which they were surrounded. Their pattern of life existed for millions of years and might have continued evermore, but nature decreed otherwise. The earth's climate changed and this Eden crumbled. There was drought. Forests disappeared. In their place stood desert and arid grassland.

Some primates retreated into what forest remained. They either became extinct or begat descendents whose playful antics now entertain us at zoos and circuses. One primate, *Australopithicus,* a sixty-pound, short, slow weakling tried to eek out an existence on the newly formed savannahs. In a while, his descendents dominated every fish, fowl, mammal, and reptile. Under pressures from their surrounding ecology and equipped with certain essential biological endowments, they forged a force which eventually overwhelmed all of earth's other inhabitants and began a compelling evolutionary trend toward the emergence of a new species, *Homo sapiens,* possessing an unparalleled capacity for experiencing empathy, forming bonds of *we,* and acting selflessly on another's behalf.

We Can Do It

Aid in developing an "imaginative reconstruction"[1] of how early hominids like *Australopithicus* forged this force and coped with the problems of survival in the ecology of a savannah exists in studies of other primates who faced similar difficulties. The use of this information in order to make inferences about the life of early "man" has been commented on by such noted scholars as F. P. G. Aldrich-Blake. He writes: ". . . much of the earlier work on primates in the 1950's was carried out by people whose prime interest was in making inferences to the social evolution of man. It was thought that animals living in a habitat comparable to that of early man would provide the greatest insight into the problems faced by our simean forebears. Under the circumstances concentration of research on open country primates was a perfectly reasonable strategy."[2]

Recent studies of baboons and chimpanzees indicate that these two normally vegetarian animals become carnivorous when living in ecological circumstances similar to those experienced by our earliest ancestors. They do so not by nibbling like scavengers on the remains of carrion left by predators, but by hunting and killing small game.[3] Of course, for *Australopithicus* and other early hominids, hunting in open country was a dangerous and difficult pursuit. Small game were ordinarily fleet, large game were often powerful as well as fleet,[4] and there were other predators, as evidenced by archeological finds at Swartkrans, South Africa.[5]

Swartkrans is something of an ancient garbage dump. It contains the remains of many thousands of animals and several primates called *Australopithicus robustus,* another manlike creature. After some investigation of the find, C. K. Brain surmised that this collection of bones was donated to science by generations of feline predators. Without intending to be beneficent, they brought their captured prey to this spot, climbed a tree to escape competitors, ate, and let the bones fall where they might. They fell into a lime deposit and were preserved. The delectability of our species and its status as prey are testified to by one other bit of evidence at Swartkrans. At least one true man, *Homo erectus,* was eaten and his bones deposited with the rest.

The dangers of hunting in prehistoric times are also evident in cave art found at Val del Charco in the Spanish Levant.[6] One scene depicts an archer fleeing from a wounded bovine. For *Australopithicus* and other early hominids the dangers were even greater than the ones faced by this prehistoric archer. They had no bows and arrows or any weapon that allowed them to greatly magnify the striking force of a weapon beyond their own physical strength; nor was it possible for them to strike a potentially fatal blow from a safe distance. Bows and arrows and spear throwers (a kind of hand-held catapult) are relatively recent inventions, not more than fifty thousand years old. By the time they were in use, humans had survived approximately three million years of predators and hunger. Stones thrown as missiles and hand-held, like axes, and sharpened sticks and bones were man's total arsenal all during this period. The array is not impressively lethal. Indeed, although there is evidence that *Australopithicus* fashioned tools,[7] it is not absolutely clear that they used these crudely worked stones and bones as weapons. Even if that were the case, as Raymond A. Dart[8] and Robert Ardrey[9] claim, it is evident that in a one-to-one squabble, a simply honed hand-held object was no match for the speed, strength and savage "weapons" of the game that these men hunted or the predators who, in turn, hunted them.

Australopithine tools or weapons are significant not because their availability quickly transformed "men" into efficient hunters; nor, as Robert Ardrey seems to insist, are they significant because they provide unequivocal evidence of man's primordial killer instincts.[10] The existence of tool manufacture and use is important because it is evidence of a mentality and intellect that was capable of planning and abstract thinking. In order to prepare a tool one must conceive of its use in situations which are *not* occurring; one must look at an object, a stone or bone, and imagine what is *not* there; one must organize immediate next steps with a remembrance of things past and an anticipation of what is yet to come. In order to prepare a tool, there must be a representation in *me* of organisms, places, and things that are not concurrently in the physical environment, in the here and now.[11]

The capacity to plan and think abstractly provided hominids with a selective advantage. And, as I will demonstrate, the *ability to transcend the here and now* is an essential element of the one force that early "man" could create in order to improve his chances at survival in open grasslands: our ancestors survived and prevailed, first on savannahs, then throughout the world, because they forged themselves into *cooperative social organizations.*[12]

Forest life allowed primates to forage for food and climb trees for safety. Young and old, male and female, all had to fend for themselves,[13] which was possible because of nature's bounty and the rapid motor development of nonhuman primates. Integrated social life was minimal. But life in savannahs for humans was harsh, and required something different. Egoistic self-sufficiency was not functional. If one had to hunt in order to eat, then pregnant females, mothers with young children, and the youngsters themselves would have quickly starved. Even the hunt was an uncertain and precarious event, and if present-day hunting societies provide a valid clue, then we must assume that a large part of the caloric intake for all group members, including the hunters, depended upon women and children gathering grubs, roots, and other edibles.[14] Because of the ecological change that had occurred, survival for our early ancestors, who possessed no natural weapons, required changes in social behaviors: defense against predators in open country, caring for the young, and hunting all required *cooperative social organization.*

Other species form social groups and cooperate. Both intraspecies and interspecies comparisons indicate that primates who spend their time in open country tend to form larger, more cohesive social

groups than those who live in forests.[15] Wolves engage in cooperative hunting and provide females and cubs who are unable to hunt
with a share of the kill. But in hominids the development of cooperative social organization as a behavioral adaptation exploited and
furthered the development of humanity's unique biological possession: a brain with the intellectual capacity and mentality that was
manifested in the manufacture and use of tools. Together, behavioral adaptation and biological endowment ignited a selective force
which fueled the development of a capacity for empathy, the necessary prerequisite for developing an *effective* cooperative social organization. It is this capacity that allows human beings to experience
the bonds of *we* and the barriers of *they;* and it is this capacity that
regulates the occurrence of altruism and aggression, benevolence
and brutality, kindness and cruelty.

Empathy, Effectiveness, and Evolution

Once I stood at the rim of the Grand Canyon fighting hard to
undo a disillusioning feeling that the panorama was unreal, a giant
billboard placed there for the pleasure of tourists. Its enormity, its
beauty, its meaning were too great for me to comprehend without
an intense, reflective, and prolonged involvement. From time to
time, the grandeur of evolution has created similar experiences for
me. It covers a time span so vast that it becomes unreal. Yet the
elegance of the process, with its slow, steady, superbly organized,
logical flow is only fully revealed if one absorbs the immense time
involved. Six-hundred million years ago is the point in time at
which we date the first fossilized animals. Two-hundred *million* years
later, amphibians emerge and they are quickly followed (in only fifty
million years) by the first reptiles. The date is not one thousand
B.C., one-hundred thousand B.C., nor even one million B.C. It is
three-hundred and forty-five million B.C. Nearly two-hundred million more years pass before reptiles cease to rule the earth and
mammals begin their ascendence. Monkeys and apes appeared
rather recently, only thirty-six million years ago. And thirty-two or
thirty-three million years later "man" trod onto the savannahs.

For nearly six-hundred million years, evolutionary changes crept
ahead slowly, methodically, until the emergence of "man." Then, in
a matter of three million years, a flash of time in terms of evolutionary clockwork, an anatomical structure as complex as the human

brain underwent an incredible three-fold increase in size. Professor Robert Bigelow of the University of Canterbury, New Zealand comments:

> Since the increase in brain size was rapid, the selective force must have been powerful. We know this powerful selective force was concentrated on the lines that led to modern man. . . . This powerful distinctively human selective force seems to have been generated within the human line itself—and since the brain functions as a social instrument, the selective force seems to have been related to distinctively human social interactions.[16]

I believe that the advent of cooperative social organization played a central role in this rapid evolution of the brain. It was part of a magnificent, but paradoxical evolutionary spiral in which cooperative social organization was first possible because a unique, more effective brain was available, and then, turning full circle, it exerted a selective force which led to the emergence of larger, still more effective brains. The reason for this spiral is simple: the prerequisites to creating an effective social organization were contingent upon empathic ability, which was, in turn, improved by the kind of intellectual capacity for abstraction that existed in the larger, more effective brains possessed by the humans who survived because they were more effective at organizing cooperatively.

In order to be effective, cooperative organizations require coordination and communication among their members; they require that everyone accept and understand the division of labor and calibrate their behavior to the behavior of others so that separate performances of interdependent tasks mesh and lead to success, not chaos; they require interpersonal trust—faith that if one becomes vulnerable by performing certain tasks which are necessary for group success, other group members will act benevolently, not malevolently. Without these qualities, a social group cannot act as one.

Thus, the life-giving functions that were characteristic of prehistoric hominid brains were not simply those associated with solving the technological problems of early social life, such as tool building. In order to act as one, group members had to possess other intellectual skills. Coordination, meaningful communication, and cooperation cannot occur unless individuals are able to transcend the *here* and *now* of their physical senses. They must be able to *take the role of an other* and look at the world by accurately assuming an other's attitude or posture.

George Herbert Mead, a noted scholar who lived in the early part of this century, said,

> The gesture that affects another, when it is a vocal gesture, is one which may have the tendency to influence the speaker as it influences others. The common expression of this is that a man knows what he is saying when the meaning of what he is saying comes to him as really as it goes to another. He is affected just as the other is. If the meaning of what he says affects the other, it affects himself in the same way. The result is that the individual who speaks, in some sense takes the attitude of the other whom he addresses. . . . It is through this sort of participation, *this taking the attitudes of other individuals, that the peculiar character of human intelligence is constituted* [italics added]. [17]

And again, in addressing the same issue more broadly, he observed, ". . . the complex co-operative processes and activities and institutional functionings of organized human society are also possible only insofar as every individual involved in them or belonging to that society can take the *general attitudes of all other such individuals* with reference to these processes and activities and institutional functionings and to the organized social whole of experiential relations and interactions thereby constituted—and can direct his own behavior accordingly [italics added]." [18]

Better brains made it possible for humans to be effectively interdependent. They did so not only by supporting tool and weapon development [19] but also by providing group members with an "ability to interpret postures, sounds, and other signals." [20] Professor Bigelow reasons that

> There was a direct link between genes, brains, interpretation, communication, cooperation, and reproductive success. . . . The circumstances which favored even more effective brains were thus built into the species itself. With each genetic advance in mental capacities in one area, the force of selection against less advanced groups in other areas became more severe. Waves of progressively more advanced groups diffused outward from the more fertile areas (for which competition was most intense) and placed increasingly severe pressures on peripheral groups whose levels of cooperation were inadequate for effective self-defense. [21]

Big, effective brains with a capacity for empathic thought provided hominids with an ever-increasing social capacity to act as one, and that capacity placed a selective advantage on big, effective brains that possessed a capacity for empathic thought.

Empathy, the capacity to take the role of an other, to reflect upon the representation of *you* in *me,* is a kind of social intelligence and a necessary element in the equation of human evolution. Unless one is possessed by instinctive controls such as those which exist in ants and bees, a social capacity to act as one cannot occur without empathy. Cooperative ties are born only when people recognize their common interests—an interlocking of their fates which will cause them to sink or swim together. Competitive ties are born, similarly, when people recognize their opposing interests.[22] In order to first comprehend cooperative or competitive ties, and then use that comprehension in order to predict another's behavior and anticipate that it will be beneficial or harmful to one's welfare, requires the social perspective granted to us by our empathic capacity. It requires the ability to accurately represent the *you* in *me,* and examine the world from another's perspective. Without that empathic capacity there can be no coordination, communication, division of labor, trust, or cooperative social organization. Without it our *genus* would be part of the litter in nature's graveyard of evolutionary mistakes. With that fundamental capacity we not only survived, but were endowed with an ability to experience both bonds of *we* and barriers of *they.*

Our empathic capacity, bequested to us through an evolutionary chain more than three million years long, is what makes it possible for us to look upon other men and women and identify them as friend or foe, as *we* or *they.* It is this bit of inherited social intelligence, combined with our other intellectual capacities that causes us to be the only creature in all the world who is capable of using abstract social cues such as race, religion, and politics to mentally divide others of our species into groups and then decide that we ourselves are or are not members of the same groups. The bonds of *we* and barriers of *they* that spring from this uniquely human form of social intelligence are what determines whether we are altruistic or aggressive.

This view of human evolution bears upon a debate that is quietly raging among ethologists, biologists, genetists, and psychologists over whether altruistic dispositions are capable of being genetically transmitted. Some, like Wynne-Edwards[23] and R. L. Trivers[24] argue cogently for the natural selection of traits which enhance the survival of a group, even at the expense of individual members. Others, for example George Williams, in his book *Adaptation and Natural Selection*,[25] object to this view, appealing to a statistical theory of evolution developed by J. B. S. Haldane which argues that the process of natural selection cannot favor the selection of dispositions which inhibit the procreational possibilities of individual group members. Stated simply, if there were a gene for self-sacrifice, then all its carriers would be too busy getting killed to procreate, thereby removing it from the genetic pool.

The debate is misguided. *Homo sapiens* is neither instinctively altruistic nor aggressive. We are not the instruments for expressing any uncontrolled primordial impulse to help or harm. Of course we have the capacity for both forms of behavior, but their expression is regulated by a capacity which was inherited because it had a selective advantage, namely the capacity for empathically experiencing oneself as part of a cooperative social unit, as part of *we*.

An instinctive impulse to behave aggressively would have been a distinct disadvantage to these early hunting societies whose survival depended on group cohesion. As Ashley Montagu said, the circumstances of life for early hominids "placed a very high premium upon his ability to co-operate. Human populations were very small, of the order of ten to one hundred individuals. In such hunting, food-gathering societies, *mutual aid* and *involvement in the welfare of others* (italics added) were not only highly valued but absolutely indispensable if the group was to survive. . . . Hence it is highly improbable that anything remotely resembling an instinct of aggression would have developed, not to mention an instinct for territoriality."[26] Early man's survival was contingent on cooperation, not aggression.

Just as coordination, communication, and the occurrence of interpersonal trust in cooperative social organizations all required the development of an empathic capacity, so too was it required for the suppression of intergroup aggression. Research presented throughout this book has repeatedly demonstrated how human beings are predisposed to experience empathically induced distress upon witnessing the plight of a *we*-group member. It is this response which prompts not only aid but also an avoidance of harming *we*-group members with whom one is cooperatively linked. No such deterring distress is experienced upon witnessing the plight of those who are not bound to us in *we*. Perhaps when others are identified as *they*, we experience them as if they were members of another species; a kind of pseudospeciation occurs and aggression is possible.

Clearly, Konrad Lorenz, the leading scholarly advocate of a model which caricatures man as a creature who is dominated by aggressive instincts, recognized the role of empathy and we-group bonds in suppressing aggression when he wrote, "I have already said that we can learn much from demagogues who pursue the opposite purpose, namely to make people fight. They know very well that personal acquaintance, indeed every kind of brotherly feeling for the people to be attacked, constitutes a strong obstacle to aggression. Every militant ideology in history has propagated the belief that the members of the other party are not quite human. . . ."[27]

Clearly human beings kill other human beings. They do so now, and have done so throughout the ages. In 1969, *Current Anthropology* carried an article by M. K. Roper entitled, "A survey of the evidence for infrahuman killing in the Pleistocene."[28] (The Pleistocene is a geological time period which covered approximately two and one-half million years, ending about ten thousand years ago, after the last glaciation.) Roper reports that at least one or more experts who examined the remains of 169 pre-*Homo sapiens,* judged fifty-six of them, 34 percent, to have injuries which could have resulted from infrahuman violence. In the Olduvai Gorge in Africa, archeologists have found the remains of a juvenile *Australopithicus* who died 1.75 million years ago from a blow to the head. He may have been murdered; he was almost certainly cannibalized. This example of ancient barbarism is not an isolated case. At the Krapina cave in Yugoslavia the skeletons of more than twenty male and female, young and old, Neanderthals were found, all cannibalized. As the author of one text comments, "One cannot escape the impression that strangers were still apt to be viewed as game animals at this time."[29]

But not everyone is a stranger. In ancient times, as now, encounters with *we* were different from encounters with *they.* Examples of ancient altruism are also evident in the bones of our ancestors. Two individuals found at a famous archeological site called Choukoutien were over fifty years of age. They lived and died more than one-hundred thousand years before our species, *Homo sapiens,* emerged. During that time, hunting without terribly effective weapons was still an essential activity. Some interpret the advanced age of these individuals as suggesting that, in those difficult times, old people were cared for.

The famous Shanidar cripple is another example of ancient altruism. Technically, the cripple, found at the Shanidar cave in Iraq, is known as Mousterian skeleton Number 1. The individual's bones reveal that he lived at least through the time it takes for an *amputation* of the right arm (below the elbow) to heal. That required aid from his fellows, especially because the amputation occurred when the victim was comparatively old. Forty-five thousand years ago, among the Neanderthals of Iraq, humans selflessly cared for one another.

Altruism and aggression have been with us since the dawn of human evolution. But, we have no *need* to be altruistic or aggressive. Humans are not subject to gushing surges of primordial instincts demanding fulfillment. We are not bladders that must be periodically relieved of a steadily amassing quantity of altruistic or aggressive material. The occurrence of altruism and aggression is regulated by the human brain's empathic capacity, which is there because it figured mightily in the survival of our species.

The drama of human evolution which gave rise to a brain with empathic capacity is symbolically recapitulated in the development of individual human beings. In the beginning, an infant's world is an egocentric blur bounded on all sides by physical senses. Even as speech and other intellectual functions develop during the early years of life there is a predominant egocentrism in sensory-motor intelligence[30] and moral judgment.[31] Ask young children to describe the appearance of an object from an angle other than the one that they occupy, and they will be unable to do so. Ask them to describe a figure to someone who cannot see it and has never seen it, and they use private, idiosyncratic references, as if all the world shared their experience. The subjective reality of their senses and experiences is accepted as the subjective reality of others. Others are not readily comprehended as separate beings who possess their own experiential world. There is no empathy.

The morality of young children fits neatly into this overall egoistic process. The world-famous developmental psychologist Jean Piaget identifies it as a period of moral realism. During this period acts are judged as good or bad because they conform or fail to conform to the letter of the law which is set by an authority. At this stage of moral development children do not consider an actor's motives or social circumstances in judging the actions of others.

By the time children enter the early grades of primary school this state of affairs begins to change. Children's moral judgments are responsive to another's motive and circumstance; a sense of justice replaces the blind demand for obedience to rule. Unwarranted generalizations rooted in the subjective reality of one's physical senses and experience begin to give way to pressures from the surrounding world: "It is only through contact with the judgments and evaluations of others that this intellectual and affective anomy will gradually yield to the pressure of collective logical and moral laws."[32] And at the center of the social process stimulating this change, says Piaget, is *cooperation and solidarity among peers.* Like our ancestors, children undergo a metamorphosis because they enter into cooperatively toned reciprocal relationships with their equals. Sustaining these relationships demands awareness of *another's* reality.

In the ordinary course of events, humans emerge from childhood with a capacity to take the role of another and decide whether they are "for us" or "agin' us," whether they are *we* or *they.* Placement in these categories is not automatically fixed by another's scent or the redness of their underbellies. It is flexibly determined by social facts, not rigidly set by biological ones. We are the one creature both gifted and burdened with the ability to allow prejudice and stereotyping, stimulated by abstract social cues like race and religion, to guide our determination of who is *we* and who is *they.* Because we are capable of making both these determinations, it is wrong to say that man is *by nature* either altruistic or aggressive. He is neither, but has the capacity for both. Indeed, because we are able to experience both the bonds of *we* and the barriers of *they,* human beings are potentially the cruelest and kindest animals on earth.

Notes

1. This creative phrase was used by S. L. Washburn and V. Avis in their chapter entitled "Evolution of Human Behavior," which appeared in Anne Roe and George Gaylord Simpson, eds., *Behavior and Evolution* (New Haven: Yale University Press, 1958).

2. F. P. G. Aldrich-Blake, "Problems of Social Structure in Forest Monkeys," in John Hurrell Crook, ed., *Social Behavior in Birds and Mammals: Essays on the Social Ethology of Animals and Man* (London: Academic Press, Inc., 1970), p. 80.

3. C. Carpenter, "A Field Study in Siam of the Behavior and Social Relations of the Gibbon, *Hylobates lar.*" *Comparative Psychology Monographs*, 16, no. 1 (1940); I. DeVore and K. Hall, "Baboon Ecology," in Irven DeVore, ed., *Primate Behavior*. (New York: Holt, Rinehart & Winston, Inc., 1965); J. Goodall, "Chimpanzees of the Gombe Stream Reserve," in DeVore, *Primate Behavior*. K. R. L. Hall, "Aggression in Monkey and Ape Societies," in John D. Carthy and Francis J. Ebling, eds., *The Natural History of Aggression* (New York: Academic Press, Inc., 1966); S. L. Washburn, P. C. Jay, and J. B. Lancaster, "Field Studies of Old World Monkeys and Apes," in Sherwood L. Washburn, ed., *Social Life of Early Man* (Chicago: Aldine Books, 1961).

4. Lewis Leakey, *Olduvai Gorge, Volume I: 1951–1961, A Preliminary Report on the Geology and Fauna* (Cambridge, Eng.: Cambridge University Press, 1967); Mary Leakey, *Olduvai Gorge, Volume III: Excavations in Beds I and II, 1960–1963.* (Cambridge, Eng.: Cambridge University Press, 1971).

5. C. K. Brain, "New Finds at the Swartkrans Australopithecine," 225 *Nature*, (1970), 1112–18.

6. L. Pericot, "The Social Life of Spanish Paleolithic Hunters as Shown by Levantine Art," in Washburn, ed., *Social Life.*

7. John E. Pfeiffer, *The Emergence of Man* (New York: Harper & Row, Publishers, 1969); S. L. Washburn, "Tools and Human Evolution," in William S. Laughlin and Richard H. Osborne, *Human Variation and Origins* (San Francisco: W. H. Freeman and Co., Publishers, 1967). For discussion of anatomical concomitants of tool manufacture and use see Wilfred Le Gros Clark, *Man-apes or Ape-men?* (New York: Holt, Rinehart & Winston, Inc., 1967). Wilfred Le Gros Clark, *The Fossil Evidence for Human Evolution* (Chicago: University of Chicago Press, 1967); J. Napier, "Fossil Hard Bones from Olduvai Gorge," *Nature* (1962), 196–409.

8. Raymond A. Dart, *Adventures with the Missing Link* (New York: Viking Press, 1959); R. A. Dart, "The Bone Tool Manufacturing Ability of Australopithicus Prometheus," *American Anthropologist*, 62, no. 134 (1960); R. A. Dart, "On the Osteodontokeratic Culture of the Australopithicine," *Current Anthropology*, 12, no. 233 (1971).

9. Robert Ardrey, *African Genesis* (New York: Atheneum, 1961).

10. Ardrey, Ibid; Ardrey, *The Territorial Imperative* (New York: Dell Publishing Co., 1966).

11. K. Oakley, "Tools Makyth Man," *Antiquity*, 31, no. 199 (1957); Washburn, "Tools."

12. For discussion of the activities of social carnivores and the advantages of cooperation, see G. Schaller, "Predators of the Serengeti: Part 2," *Natural History*, 81, no. 60 (1972); George Schaller, *The Serengeti Lion: A Study of Predator-Prey Relations* (Chicago: University of Chicago Press, 1972); G. Schaller and G. Lowther, "The Relevance of Carnivore

Behavior to the Study of Early Hominids," *Southwestern Journal of Anthropology*, 25, no. 307 (1969). For speculations about the size and structure of early hominid groups, see J. Birdsell, "Some Predictions for the Pleistocene Based on Equilibrium Systems Among Recent Hunter-gatherers," in Richard B. Lee and Irven DeVore, eds., *Man the Hunter* (Chicago: Aldine Publishing Co., 1968).

13. A. I. Hallowell, "The Proto Cultural Foundations of Human Adaptations," in Washburn, *Social Life*.

14. Alexander Alland, Jr., *The Human Imperative* (New York: Columbia University Press, 1972).

15. M. R. A. Chance, "The Nature and Special Features of the Instinctive Social Bond of Primates," in Washburn, *Social Life*; I. DeVore, "A Comparison of the Ecology and Behavior of Monkeys and Apes," in Sherwood L. Washburn, ed., *Classification and Human Evolution* (New York: Viking Fund Publications, 1963); Lionel Tiger, *Men in Groups* (New York: Vintage Press, 1970).

16. R. Bigelow, "The Evolution of Cooperation, Aggression, and Self-control," *1972 Nebraska Symposium on Motivation*, 20 (1973), 1–59.

17. George H. Mead, *On Social Psychology*, edited by Anselm Strauss (Chicago: University of Chicago Press, 1964), p. 37.

18. G. H. Mead, Ibid, p. 219.

19. Washburn, "Tools."

20. Bigelow, "The Evolution," p. 3.

21. Bigelow, Ibid, p. 4.

22. Morton Deutsch, *The Resolution of Conflict* (New Haven: Yale University Press, 1973), especially part one.

23. V. C. Wynne-Edwards, *Animal Dispersion in Relation to Social Behavior* (Edinburgh: Oliver and Boyd, 1962).

24. R. L. Trivers, "The Evolution of Reciprocal Altruism," *Quarterly Review of Biology*, 46 (1971), 35–37.

25. George C. Williams, *Adaptation and Natural Selection* (Princeton, N.J.: Princeton University Press, 1966); also D. T. Campbell, "On the Genetics of Altruism and the Counter-hedonic Components of Human Culture," *Journal of Social Issues, 28, no. 3 (1972)*, 21–38.

26. The quote appeared in the *Los Angeles Times*, May 26, 1968; for similar conclusions see Theodore Dobzhansky, *Mankind Evolving: The Evolution of the Human Species* (New Haven: Yale University Press, 1962).

27. Konrad Lorenz, *On Aggression* (New York: Bantam Books, Inc., 1967), p. 273.

28. M. K. Roper, "A Survey of the Evidence for Intrahuman Killing in the Pleistocene," *Current Anthropology*, 10 (1969), 427–59.

29. Chester S. Chard, *Man in Prehistory* (New York: McGraw-Hill Book Company, 1969).

30. Jean Piaget, *The Origins of Intelligence in Children* (New York: International Universities Press, 1952); Jean Piaget, *The Construction of Reality in the Child* (New York: Basic Books, Inc., Publishers, 1954).

31. Jean Piaget, *The Moral Judgment of the Child* (New York: The Free Press, 1965).

32. J. Piaget, Ibid, p. 401.

5

Infrahuman animals and altruism:
everybody's doin' it

Three large male baboons from the troop sat themselves down on the stone wall which formed a semicircle around the car. Their heads turned in every direction but one, toward us. It was almost as if they were *pretending* not to notice. Had they been human, I would say that they were performing some antiquated vaudeville routine which was always too transparent to be funny. You know the bit: "Hey Charlie, you see anything going on?" "No, Harry. Do you?" "No, I don't. How about you, Sam. Do you see anything goin' on?" "Me. I don't see anything. Why, do you?" And so on, until some subliminal cue from the audience tells the performer that it is time to change the gag.

The rest of the troop, being less theatrically inclined, was spread out for three or four yards along the stone wall. Some were watching us, others were idly gamboling, and a few were picking fruit from the lush vegetation. Everything was right: the baboons, the vegetation, and the Indian Ocean shimmering far below, filling the background to the horizon. It all assembled into a splendidly unique collage titled *Africa*.

While some of my friends climbed from the automobile in order to take photographs, my attention was drawn to a very small baboon riding on a female, almost certainly his mother. He was boney, with a too-large head, bulging eyes, and skin that seemed to fit rather badly.

After a few moments, with no agility whatsoever, this little fellow climbed down from his mother and, for no apparent reason, raced clumsily back and forth along the stone wall. His mother, looking for fresh pickings, dropped from the wall onto the road just as the car's engine was started. As we moved very slowly forward, the baby, possibly frightened, leaped from the wall for his mother's back. Unfortunately, at that very second, she was vaulting back to the wall. They crashed midway, and the baby plunged to the road-way on his back, screaming. With a howl, the mother rushed back down, grabbed the infant, and fled up to the wall, where the three males now awaited her. There they sat, with the mother cradling and rocking the screaming baby and the males glaring directly at us.

It all happened so suddenly that my friends missed seeing parts of the incident and it was quickly replaced by other topics of conversation. But the event stubbornly dominated my thoughts. The highway that we were driving along rimmed the southernmost edge of Africa, the continent on which human life probably had its beginnings. After a moment or two, I looked away from the sea, up to the surrounding cliffs, which were sometimes barren and sometimes shrouded in exotic foliage, and wondered. . . Was that simple, almost instantaneous event truly a fundamental illustration of a living thing's capacity to care about the plight of others? Was it a pure, primitive, unblemished example of selflessness and concern?

The answers to these questions are complex. Gulls scream at the sight of predators, causing their young to remain safely still; rats urinate a warning signal on poisoned bait; geese band together in joint territorial defense; and chimpanzees engage in solicited and unsolicited food sharing. Are these events acceptable illustrations of altruism in infrahuman species? No! The term *altruism* must be reserved for acts which are purposive responses to another's actual or impending distress.

Obviously, this definitional criterion creates new problems. Determining whether an animal's behavior is being regulated by another's actual or impending distress is not an easy matter. Animals are simply unable to respond to interviewer's questions with an articulate, in-depth analysis of their motivational states. Professors Donald O. Hebb and Walter R. Thompson, two of the world's foremost comparative psychologists, comment on this problem. The difficulty of identifying purposive behavior in infrahuman species, they say,

". . . is that it may have to be seen repeatedly in order to be sure that its objective is achieved neither accidentally nor mechanically."[1] Purposive behavior varies with circumstance; it is not a consistent, robotlike reaction that is unmindful of changing conditions. Warnings are purposive if they are made *only* when another animal is endangered and they stop when the other is safe. In short, the act's beginning and end must be determined by the other's condition of distress. Gulls scream at the sight of predators even when there is no one around to hear them. The scream is therefore reflexive. It is emotional expression. Although it may produce protective immobility in chicks, it cannot be considered altruistic.

Because altruism has so many cleverly disguised imposters, natural observation of behavior can be misleading. As the gull's warning scream illustrates, seemingly altruistic behavior sometimes occurs as a *reflexive response* to environmental stimuli. Their reaction to predators is impelled, possibly, by an inborn template of instincts. If others are helped, the altruism is no more than an *ersatz*, primitive example of the real thing. It is, what I shall call, *prototypic*.

Prototypic Altruism

I have never tasted impala, but lions have, and they like the taste, which is very unfortunate for impala. If impala have anything like "concerns," then to avoid being eaten by a lion must surely be a major one. In fact, a cursory glance at their behavior might leave the mistaken impression that impala act altruistically in order to protect one another from becoming a gastronomical event. When danger threatens they snort a warning to fellow impala. Of course, by snorting, the snorter calls attention to himself. But natural selection has bequeathed that as the possible price an individual impala must pay for species survival. In reality, the impala's snort probably lacks purposeful intent. It is a reflexive response to danger that happens to enhance other impala's chances of survival.

So it is with the Thompson gazelle, also a tasty dish to set before the king of beasts, as well as less regal predators. Gazelle do not snort, however. They stot. Stoting is leaping, stiff-legged, high into the air. It is a very adequate warning, but one that potentially jeopardizes the leaper, who is aiding his fellows by stoting reflexively at the sight of danger.

Jackdaws provide still another example of an act that cannot be considered anything more than prototypic altruism. These birds appear to come to the aid of other daws who have been captured by an enemy. In fact, on one occasion the enemy was Konrad Lorenz.[2] The daws attacked Lorenz while he was dealing with one of their fellows. This would seem to make a good case for nonprototypic jackdaw altruism but, unfortunately for Lorenz and for this argument, these birds also attacked him while he was carrying a wet black bathing suit. "Assuming that the jackdaws' visual acuity is equal to the discrimination involved, as it must be, there is no reason to suppose that either attack was a purposeful attempt to help a fellow."[3]

Impala, gazelle, and jackdaws are not properly called heroes or altruists. Nevertheless, they have been equipped by evolution to act in ways that sometimes have the incidental consequence of helping their fellows. At the sight of a predator, or a reasonable facsimile thereof, their potentially self-sacrificing response may be their only option. Human altruism is easily distinguished from these prototype examples. But set that issue aside for the moment. The essential point is that in some circumstances natural selection favors the preservation of behavior which has critical altruistic by-products because of the advantage it provides in species survival. Thus, the *capacity* for engaging in behavior that aids others may be inherited right along with such things as visual and auditory acuity.

Cooperation and Mutual Aid

Prototypic altruism is not the only imposter posing as true altruism. Some acts which seem altruistic are actually not because they are motivated by the anticipation of concrete, tangible rewards. Consider the process of social grooming among infrahuman primates.

Surely, if you and I are at all alike, one of life's great frustrations is the inability to effectively scratch your own back and other hard-to-get-at places. Rubbing up and down against doorframes, using clothes hangers, and other more ornate claw-shaped tools, usually purchased in a curio shop in some quaint section of the city all miss the mark, if you will excuse the pun. Nothing—nothing is so satisfying as a friendly hand, someone else's, digging in, up and down, moving closer to the target, as you call instructions with the precision of a spotter for artillery.

It may give you little satisfaction to learn that nonhuman primates have a similar problem, and their resolution of it parellels our own. They simply cooperate. Each animal works hard to pick through another's fur. The groomee benefits: as the grooming occurs, it probably feels good, and clean fur almost certainly produces less discomfort than dirty fur. But the rewards are not unilateral. The groomer also benefits: grooming is frequently reciprocal and it ordinarily yields small, consumable delicacies. Because there are rewards for the groomer, the process of grooming another becomes associated with pleasant experiences. In time, these associations become reward enough, and grooming might then occur even in the absence of a real need for cleaner fur or reciprocal gestures from the groomee. But this is not altruism. The act *has nothing to do* with another's welfare.[4]

Once, a substantial number of albino rats were witnesses to a sad sight. One of their brother rats was suspended in a harness, high above the floor. Hanging high in the air is unpleasant for rats and their consternation is registered with squeals and struggling. Rats seem to act altruistically in an effort to aid other rats who are in this predicament. If they are provided with a simple bar-pressing device which, when operated, lowers their distressed kin, they will learn to use it, and will do so frequently.[5] Some argue that it is a mistake to accept this bar pressing as an example of true altruistic behavior. They point to evidence which clearly shows that rats make even more bar presses to cause the cessation of "white noise" (a loud, unpleasant random static sound) than they do to cause the cessation of recorded squeals of other rats. Thus, they conclude, the seemingly altruistic bar-pressing reaction is nothing more than a self-gratifying response to noxious auditory stimuli.[6]

Their argument may have merit, but I want to alert you to an alternative one which holds the behavior of these rats to be an example of true altruism. The fact that another rat's squeals are noxious *is the point.* They are not pleasant, rewarding sounds, nor are they neutrally inconsequential ones. Rats share man's aversion to the suffering of some of their brethren. By the time these rodents were recruited by science, they disliked hearing another recruit squeal in fear. Inferring a human being's intent is difficult. Inferring a rat's intent is even more so. But in this instance that is not necessary. The fact is that rats were distressed in response to another rat's expression of distress. And, as is the case with human beings, hedonism compelled altruism. In order to stop those noxious squeals, they rescued one of their fellows from harm.

Although the conclusive experiment has not been done, it seems reasonable to speculate that rats do not respond equally to the squeals of all other rats. "What rats do when a member of a strange rat clan enters their territory or is put there by a human experimenter is one of the most horrible and repulsive things which can be observed in animals." The stranger roams about until one of the real residents smells the intruder. Then "the information is transmitted like an electric shock through the resident rat, and at once the whole colony is alarmed. . . . With eyes bulging from their sockets, their hair standing on end, the rats set out on the rat hunt." When they eventually rip the stranger into shreds, surely he squeals in distress, but the attack does not cease.[7] The odor of his coat excludes him from *we*. When the other is clearly *they*, for whatever reason, his plight provokes no pity.

We-group formation and cooperation among chimpanzees also produces behavior which is seemingly altruistic. In the early 1930s M. P. Crawford[8] taught pairs of hungry chimps to pull together on a rope in order to obtain a box containing food. Cooperation was essential because the weight of the box was too great for a single chimp to manage. Since both benefited by pulling on the rope, their individual behavior hardly qualifies as altruistic. But there came a day when the time for pulling arrived and one of the chimps was not hungry. He had had a decent meal, and as students of animal behavior say, "he was sated." Would he help the other chimp to obtain a square meal by pulling his part of the load? Yes indeed! This is frequently just what occurred. But why? Was this apparently selfless act simply an unwitting, learned response to a particular stimulus, the rope, or was it a purposive attempt to provide another with benefit? The information Crawford's experiment obtained is insufficient to answer these questions. But that should not cause us to overlook an important fact—at a minimum, this experiment and the previously mentioned one using albino rats both illustrate that some infrahuman species have the capacity to learn and engage in behavior that results in benefit for another.

In a sense I have taken the long way around to demonstrate that this capacity exists. Most of us are, or were, zoo-goers. And zoo-goers who have observed maternal behavior, particularly among infrahuman mammals, probably do not need to be convinced that animals, other than *Homo sapiens,* seem to exhibit concern for one another's welfare.

Maternal Aid and Concern

The female thread worm, *Rhabdonema nigrovenosa,* reproduces by laying eggs which hatch inside her body. Her offspring, the ungrateful wretches, then proceed to eat her insides in order to gain access to the outside world.[9] Her sacrifice is great and, symbolically, it is richly meaningful—after all, how many parents protest "You're eating out my insides!"—but it is an act that lacks intent. It is a case of prototypic altruism. The female thread worm is no altruist where her children are concerned. She is simply a passive vessel for nature's macabre solution to the problem of facilitating the survival of her species.

Maternal response patterns of large-brained infrahuman mammals are rarely as simple or invariant as this example. There is considerable anecdotal evidence which suggests that these species are capable of engaging in complex, purposeful altruistic behavior in response to unique situations. The baboon mother that I witnessed rescuing and comforting her screaming infant was exhibiting a suitably adaptive response to her child's distress. Such behavior on the part of nonhuman primates is not uncommon. Youngsters who have fallen from their perches often find themselves rescued by adult males and females who are not necessarily their parents. Adults also assist small ones to cross spaces which would be impassible without their aid.[10] These acts are not easily thought of as reflex actions such as snorting and stoting; nor do they appear to provide the helper with external, tangible rewards. Indeed, they seem very well qualified as infrahuman examples of purposive altruism in response to another's actual or impending distress.

Clarence Ray Carpenter, a famed scholar who has been described as the first person to study primate social organization, tells us several stories of maternal aid and concern among nonhuman primates. They are contained in the classic report of his observations of howler monkeys on Barro Colorado Island in the Panama Canal Zone, between December 25, 1931 and May 12, 1933.[11] The howler's voice earned this monkey his name. It pierces the air for between one and two miles.

During the 1700s, Captain William Dampier described these monkeys:[12]

> The Monkeys that are in these Parts are the ugliest I ever saw. They are bigger than a Hare, and have great Tails about two Foot and a half long. . . . These Creatures keep together 20 or 30 in a Company, and ramble over the Woods. . . . If they meet a single Person they will threaten to devour him."

When Captain Dampier first met these "ugly" beasts,

> They were a large Company dancing from Tree to Tree, over my Head; chattering and making a terrible Noise. . . . Some broke down dry Sticks and threw them at me; others scattered their Urine and Dung about my ears.

A nasty fellow is the howler monkey, although Captain Dampier should not have taken it so personally. Most monkeys urinate and defecate when excited.

Two centuries after Captain Dampier's contact with these animals, on January 23, 1933, to be exact, Clarence Ray Carpenter witnessed a sad but touching display of their capacity for maternal concern. After completing some observations, he started to return to camp when an object falling to the ground attracted his attention. He investigated and found an infant, dazed, with a bloodied nose. Male howlers, Carpenter reports, were already behaving frantically, as if searching for the infant on the ground. After a moment, the infant awoke, found itself in Carpenter's arms, and shouted a distress cry. Pandemonium broke loose. "The entire clan began to react most vigorously. The males dashed here and there and roared; an adult female with an associated juvenile behaved in frantic fashion and produced wailing vocal patterns; all individuals of the clan ceased feeding and approached nearer and nearer the ground."

Carpenter prevented the infant from climbing to its clan and eventually took it for three months of observation. As he carried it away, the previously mentioned adult female, who we must assume was the mother, followed "wailing pitifully in response to the distress cries of the infant."[13]

I believe it is reasonable to conclude that the mother's behavior is an example of altruistic concern. It appears to be more responsive to another's distress than either snorting or stoting. After all, she alone followed Carpenter as he abducted her crying child. If the act were instinctively reflexive or learned, then we would expect other animals to have behaved in the same way, or to have fled, if we choose to assume that distress cries signal danger. The other howlers did neither. Instead, they approached closer to the ground, possibly shouting their challenge. By contrast, the uniqueness and complexity of the mother's response suggests purposefulness, variation and responsiveness, born out of special ties.

In his book, the *Naturalistic Behavior of Nonhuman Primates,* Clarence Ray Carpenter reports two other observations which are extreme illustrations of maternal behavior. One of them is poignant, the other barbaric. He describes the pathetically beautiful response of two rhesus mothers when their children died. Rather than abandon their small, lifeless babies, they carried them until the tiny corpses deteriorated in their arms. This love and concern for infants is also evident in Carpenter's observations of adult male and female monkeys who "adopt" orphaned babies of their own and *other* species.

But maternal behavior of this sort is not genetically fixed and immutable. Under some circumstances, mothers will kill their children. During his career, Carpenter established a Rhesus monkey colony on the island of Santiago in Puerto Rico. While voyaging to the island from India, eight to ten of the mothers killed their own young. Indeed, during the colony's first years, more young died because they were murdered by adults than for any other reason.[14] But don't "tsk, tsk," at the monkeys; there are times when human beings also identify their own children as objects of hate and scorn. For reasons that are often irrational and unconscious the young ones are experienced as *they.* The brutality and butchering that follows is, unfortunately, a foremost cause of mortality among infants and young children.

Obviously, a mammal's *capacity* for maternal behavior must be considered as just that; it is a *potential.* Romantic conceptions of maternal instincts are fallaciously exaggerated. They are not inevitably displayed in response to strict biological demands. Among many large-brained mammals, genetic history combines with social circumstance to determine whether maternal behavior will be altruistic or aggressive.

Altruistic Behavior

Data from scientific observations in jungles and laboratories provide clear evidence of altruistic behavior among infrahumans. Robert Ardrey, recounting the observations of a British ornithologist, David Lack, tells the story of an old, white pelican who was blind. For Ardrey, for me, and perhaps for Lack as well, the most astounding fact about this unsighted bird was that he was alive. Pelicans eat fish. In fact, they dive, headfirst, for the fish they eat. That is quite a trick for a blind pelican. The pelican was alive, Ardrey surmises, because he was cared for and fed by others of his flock.[15]

This same concern for other adult members of one's group is evident among howler monkeys. Howler clans move with ease and agility from place to place through the tree tops. This leaves the occasional crippled monkey at a considerable disadvantage. Moving slowly from branch to branch, the monkey falls far behind the others, and that is dangerous. Predators lurk, and a lone monkey is a tempting target. But howlers are not unmindful of their lame comrades. C. R. Carpenter has observed crippled monkeys who lagged dangerously behind shout distress signals which caused the clan to stop, allowing them to catch up and again enjoy the group's protection.[16]

The behavior of the howlers and the pelicans are not sham examples of altruism. Unlike stoting or grooming, they are genuine examples of behavior calibrated to another's need for aid. There are many other such examples of infrahuman species purposively ministering to others of their kind.

On one occasion a female porpoise housed at Marine Studios was giving birth. The event aroused the males and one became quite aggressive. Immediately the other females formed a protective screen around the expectant mother. Their behavior was clearly directed at keeping the male at a safe distance. "When the newborn infant began its first gradual ascent to the surface to breathe, another female accompanied the mother in swimming just below the infant in readiness to support it if it had failed to make the grade."[17]

Desmond Morris, author of *The Naked Ape*, relates the story of a female chimpanzee who indicated to a nearby male her distress over a cinder that was lodged in her eye.[18] Gallantly, the male proceeded to gently examine and then remove the cinder. This was no reflex action, and reciprocity seems to me to be an extremely unlikely explanation of the behavior. This chimpanzee was acting on the female's behalf. Some might argue that this act was not truly altruistic since it was solicited. I disagree. The fact that he acted at her behest does not alter the act's purposive intent or lessen its altruistic quality; it only indicates that chimpanzees have the capacity to communicate distress.

Another example of selflessly extended medicinal care among nonhuman primates involves Ingagi and Mbongo, two male gorillas who lived at the Zoological Garden in San Diego, California. They were captured in 1930, just about the time of their fourth birthday. In 1934, C. R. Carpenter conducted an observational study of these two delightful animals. I would like to spend time recapturing a broad range of Carpenter's observations of Ingagi and Mbongo. As usual, Carpenter provided a careful, meticulous account, and the animals were charming. But I must forego the temptation to report at length on Ingagi's and Mbongo's antics, in order to concentrate on a portion of Carpenter's account which is relevant to our concern.

In August, 1934, Mbongo received a slight laceration on his left shoulder. Both Ingagi and Mbongo had received wounds before and they were observed delivering first-aid to themselves. For example, on July 19, 1934, Mbongo bruised his hand. After soothing it in his mouth, he placed it in the water basin and, using his good hand, gently sprinkled water on it. But in August, when he injured his shoulder, an area which is awkward to observe without the use of a mirror, it was Ingagi who cared for the wound. Ingagi's ministrations consisted of plucking hair from the wounded area and placing his lips to the laceration. Modern medicine might doubt the value of these practices, but of their intent there can be no question—Ingagi was deliberately providing Mbongo with aid.[19]

Aid of a different sort was witnessed by Professor Donald O. Hebb in an experiment that he conducted with chimpanzees.[20] Professor Hebb confronted the chimpanzees, Mimi and Lia, with a bold and a timid man (actually the same person but in disguise). The bold man played rough and responded to aggression with aggression. The timid man was hesitant, nervous, and withdrew at sudden moves. The chimps took advantage of the timid man. They were disobedient and, from Professor Hebb's description, I would say that they mounted a concerted effort to torment the poor fellow. Their response to the bold man was quite different.

Lia was very wary of him. Mimi, however, was a tiger of a chimp. She took no guff and repeatedly attacked. On February 14. 1944, she was doing just that when the bold man grabbed her finger and bent it. Mimi screamed, but bravely redoubled her attack. Lia, hearing Mimi's scream, joined in the attack until she got punched on the hand. That was enough for Lia. With occasional aggressive gestures toward the bold man, Lia kept trying to pull *Mimi's hands away from danger.* One week after this episode, when tough little Mimi attacked again, Hebb tells us that Lia worked hard to pull her away from the bold man.

Similar concern on the part of nonhuman primates was observed by Carpenter, who tells the story of an ocelot that lay hidden in a palm tree, patiently awaiting prey.[21] In time a juvenile howler monkey came by and was attacked. The young howler's distress cries did not cause his clan to flee. On the contrary, male adult howlers literally roared into action, rushing toward the scene of attack. Their fury must have been tremendous because the ocelot, which had already severely gashed the youngster, withdrew at full speed.

These examples were presented in order to substantiate the claim that altruism among infrahuman species does occur. Of course, as Professor Hebb has written,

> Nothing other animals do proves anything about man, but such evidence does refute the principal criticism of human data: that doctrinaire argument, that all altruism in the true sense cannot exist, that all motivation must be selfish (based ultimately on primary biological needs).[22]

In light of the generalizations made by Lorenz, Ardrey, and others, Professor Hebb's comment warrants careful attention. The truth or falsity of any proposition about human behavior cannot be based on data obtained from other animals. Analogous behavior patterns in different species cannot be regarded as equivalent. Within the limits of our knowledge about phylogenetic evolution, analysis of such patterns permits *inferences* about other species, but they *prove* nothing at all. The evolutionary origins of analogous behavior patterns may differ and the conditions which are antecedent to their occurrence may also differ. For that reason, when scientists examine the behavior of infrahuman species, the folk wisdom which advises "For instance is not proof" cannot be taken *too* seriously. Nonetheless, our conviction in theories about the causes of human behavior, including altruism, must be strengthened if corroborative evidence is available from animals lower than humans on the phylogenetic scale. Therefore, we now must delve further in an effort to determine whether infrahuman altruistic behavior occurs in a manner similar to that of human altruism. I think it does. Investigations with nonhuman primates provide strong indication that these animals have the capacity for empathy and that *we*-group members are more likely to receive help than *they*-group members!

Students of animal behavior will forever pay special tribute to the name Yerkes. It is irrevocably associated with monumental pioneering efforts in this area of scholarship. In an article published in 1935 called "Social Behavior in Infrahuman Primates," Robert M. Yerkes and Ada W. Yerkes discussed food-sharing among chimpanzees. Although it is a rather common occurrence, they said, it does not occur arbitrarily.

> Everything depends upon the nature and relations of donor and recipient and the circumstances in which the act of refusal or sharing occurs. Ordinarily there must exist a *friendly relationship, sympathy,* anxiety, pity, desire for sexual association or some comparable affective background as condition of food-sharing. Between antagonistic individuals we have *never* seen the sharing of foods or of other prized and strongly desired possessions.[23] [italics added]

This statement by the Yerkes was largely based on their observations of chimpanzees in natural settings. In 1936, Professors H. W. Nissen and M. P. Crawford published an article in the *Journal of Comparative Psychology* that reported a more systematic study of this phenomenon, which was conducted in an animal behavior laboratory.[24]

Professors Nissen and Crawford placed one chimpanzee in each of two adjoining cages. One of the chimps was deprived; he had no food, but he did have access to a vending machine that was operated by tokens: one token yielded one grape. Unfortunately, he had no tokens either. By contrast, the chimp in the adjoining cage was wealthy. He had food, which was desirable, and tokens, which were of no value to him whatsoever. (This changed in a second study where he too had a vending machine. The results of both studies, however, are the same.) For different reasons, Nissen, Crawford, and the deprived chimp all shared the same concern—how often would the affluent chimp share food and tokens?

The chimps were not stubbornly selfish. A number of tokens were shared and so was a small amount of food. Sometimes these gifts were shared in response to requests; sometimes they were given without being solicited. The affluent chimps were capable of acting on the other's behalf. But more important is an observation by Nissen and Crawford contained in their concluding comments: "Begging and positive responsiveness to begging occurred much more frequently between animals who previously had established a close friendship than among those not intimate with each other." Help was not extended indiscriminately, even when requested. It tended to be given to *we*-group members and withheld from others.

Nearly three decades after Professors Nissen and Crawford published their findings, the same pattern of *we*-group helping among nonhuman primates was observed during experiments by three researchers, J. H. Masserman, S. Wechkin, and W. Terris.[25] In the first of these experiments, fifteen rhesus monkeys, eight males and seven females, were trained to secure a small delicacy by pulling on one chain in response to a red light and another in response to a blue one. The delicacy in this case was a .7-gram pellet of food fit for monkeys.

When the monkeys learned this task, the researchers pulled a rather dirty trick. They placed another rhesus in a nearby compartment, visible to the chain-pulling rhesus. For three days all went well; .7 grams of monkey delicacy were delivered whenever the correct chain was pulled in response to the red or blue light. On the fourth day this paradise crumbled. When one of the two chains was pulled, the food was delivered, but the monkey in the adjoining cage received a very uncomfortable, high-frequency electric shock. Thus, the dilemma: if the rhesus could wonder, then, they would have to ask themselves, "Should I pull each chain on the appropriate occasion in order to receive those delicious pellets, or should I forego those goodies some of the time by pulling the chain that produces pellets without causing any distress for that poor fellow in the next cage?"

These rhesus monkeys responded to the other's plight. Ten of them showed a decided preference for the nonshock chain, and two others refused to pull either chain after seeing the other so distressed. Most importantly, the researchers report that this altruistic behavior was twice as likely to occur when the electric shock victim was a cagemate than when he was a stranger!

A second experiment produced this very same pattern. The participants in this one were ten in number, "6 male and 4 female sexually immature rhesus macaques." Their experiences were the same as the first group's. And once again, these monkeys were more likely to behave selflessly when the victim was a cagemate, someone who was familiar, a member of their we-group.

Another finding of the first experiment was also repeated: Those monkeys who had themselves experienced electric shock exhibited the strongest tendency toward engaging in selfless behavior. Is it possible that this experience provided some monkeys with a basis for more fully understanding what the victim was experiencing? The empathic capacities of nonhuman primates have been seriously investigated for some time, and the data are very convincing—without prior training, normally reared monkeys can use facial expressions and other cues emitted by fellow monkeys as guides to their own behavior.[26] In this case, a monkey's own experiences as a victim may have created an empathic bond, infusing the other victim's expressions of distress with special potency.

Nonhuman primates appear to have capacities similar to those that we find in human beings: they are empathically aroused by the plight of their fellows and show a decided preference for helping those with whom they have friendly ties. Among primates, human and nonhuman, there are repeated indications of a common theme: selfless behavior is primarily determined by surrounding social conditions, it is not rigidly regulated by an inborn template of instinctual controls.

Why should this happen? Why does altruism replace apathy when bonds of we prevail over barriers of they ? What psychological forces motivate human beings to help when fellow we-groupers are in need of aid? What is the psychology of selflessness?

In order to answer these questions we must leave the exotic jungles and animal laboratories and journey back in time nearly one-half century to a cafe in Berlin.

Notes

1. D. O. Hebb and W. R. Thompson, "The Social Significance of Animal Studies," in Gardner Lindzey and Elliot Aronson, eds., *The Handbook of Social Psychology, Volume II* (Reading, Mass.: Addison Wesley, 1968), p. 739.

2. K. Lorenz, "A Contribution to the Comparative Sociology of Colonial-nesting Birds," *Proceedings of the International Ornithological Congress*, 8 (1934), 207–18.

3. Hebb and Thompson, Ibid, p. 743.

4. For discussions of grooming see Irvin DeVore, *Primate Behavior* (New York: Holt, Rinehart & Winston, Inc., 1965); Desmond Morris, *The Naked Ape* (New York: Dell, 1967); J. Sparks, "Social Grooming in Animals," *New Scientist* (1963), 253–57; Lionel Tiger, *Man in Groups* (New York: Random House, Inc., Vintage Books, 1970).

5. G. E. Rice, Jr. and P. Gainer, " 'Altruism' in the Albino Rat," *Journal of Comparative and Physiological Psychology*, 55 (1962), 123–25; G. E. Rice, Jr., "Aiding Responses in Rats: Not in Guinea Pigs," paper printed at the meeting of the American Psychological Association, Chicago, Ill., September, 1965.

6. J. J. Lavery and P. J. Foley, "Altruism or Arousal in the Rat?" *Science*, 140 (1963), 172–73.

7. Konrad Lorenz, *On Aggression* (New York: Bantam Books, Inc., 1966), chapter ten.

8. M. P. Crawford, "The Cooperative Solving of Problems by Young Chimpanzees," *Comparative Psychology Monographs*, 14, no. 68 (1973), 1–88, (entire issue).

9. S. J. Holmes, "The Reproductive Beginnings of Altruism," *Psychological Bulletin*, 52 (1945), 109–12.

10. F. P. G. Aldrich-Blake, "Problems of Social Structure in Forest Monkeys," in John Hurrell Crook, ed., *Social Behavior in Birds and Mammals: Essays on the Social Ethology of Animals and Man* (London: Academic Press, Inc., 1970).

11. C. R. Carpenter, "A Field Study of the Behavior and Social Relations of Howling Monkeys," *Comparative Psychology Monographs*, 10, no. 2 (1934), p. 48.

12. Carpenter, Ibid.

13. Carpenter, Ibid, p. 72–75.

14. Clarence R. Carpenter, *Naturalistic Behavior of Nonhuman Primates* (University Park, Penn.: The Pennsylvania State University Press, 1964).

15. Robert Ardrey, *The Social Contract* (New York: Dell Publishing Co., Inc., Delta Books, 1971).

16. Carpenter, "A Field Study."

17. A. F. McBride and D. O. Hebb, "Behavior of the Captive Bottle-nose Dolphin, *Tursiops truncatus,*" *Journal of Comparative and Physiological Psychology*, 41 (1948), 111–23.

18. Morris, *The Naked Ape.*

19. Carpenter, *Naturalistic Behavior.*

20. Hebb and Thompson, "The Social Significance."

21. Carpenter, "A Field Study."

22. D. O. Hebb, "Comment on Altruism: The Comparative Evidence," *Psychological Bulletin*, 76, no. 6 (1971), p. 409.

23. R. M. Yerkes and A. W. Yerkes, "Social Behavior of Infrahuman Primates," in Clark Murchison, ed., *A Handbook of Social Psychology*, (Worcester, Mass.: Clark University Press, 1935).

24. H. W. Nissen and M. P. Crawford, "A Preliminary Study of Food-sharing Behavior in Young Chimpanzees," *Journal of Comparative Psychology*, 22 (1936), 383–419.

25. J. H. Masserman, S. Wechkin, and W. Terris, Jr., "Altruistic Behavior in Rhesus Monkeys," *American Journal of Psychiatry*, 121 (1964), 584–85; S. Wechkin, J. R. Masserman, and W. Terris, Jr., "Shock to a Conspecific as an Aversive Stimulus, *Psychonomic Service*, 1 (1964), 47–48.

26. I. A. Mirsky, R. E. Miller, and J. V. Murphy, "The Communication of Affect in Rhesus Monkeys: I. An Experimental Method," *Journal of the American Psychoanalytic Association*, 6 (1958), 433–40; R. E. Miller, W. F. Caul, and I. A. Mirsky, "Communication of Affects Between Feral and Socially Isolated Monkeys," *Journal of Personality and Social Psychology*, 7, no. 3 (1967), 231–39.

6

A small cafe in Berlin

World War One had ended, Kaiser Wilhelm's "threat" to the safety
of democracy was crushed, and, in America, the "Roaring Twenties" was about to begin. "These were the days, my friend." It was
1921, and Kurt Lewin had just received an appointment to the faculty of the University of Berlin. "Appointment" is really a euphe-
mism. *Privatdozent* ("private lecturer") was the title that Lewin actually received. As a *Privatdozent* he lectured, but for no fixed salary.
Privatdozents received a portion of student fees, and their income depended on the popularity of their lectures. As a faculty member of
a large university, I can only emit a cartoonist's "GULP" at the
prospect of this arrangement. Many of my colleagues are probably
"gulping" right along with me. Few of us would like to "sing for
our supper" in this way. But Kurt Lewin had few options. He was
young and Jewish, and his *Privatdozent* role was not an unfamiliar
one in 1921 at the University of Berlin.

According to his biographer and friend, Alfred J. Marrow,[1] Lewin
fared reasonably well in this environment. He was not a great ora-
tor, but he was intellectually stimulating. His ideas were unconven-
tional and his excitement about them contagious. "At the start we
were not greatly impressed by his lecturing, for Lewin was in no
way a polished or outstanding speaker and we had been spoiled by
the brilliant lectures of Kohler and others," said Dr. Vera Mahler.[2]

87

But after a short while attitudes changed. "We would sit in our seats . . . completely absorbed, as Lewin began to develop his train of thought. I shouldn't say he lectured—he really didn't in a conventional, well-organized manner. He was often creating as he was speaking. Frequently he paused in mid-sentence and seemed to forget his audience. Thinking aloud, he invented the new ideas pouring quickly into his mind."

Students began to gather about Lewin. Outside of class they met regularly at the Schwedische Cafe, located near the University. Hour upon hour they would sit, sipping coffee, eating cakes, and arguing about psychology. In time their meetings at the Cafe became known as *Quasselstrippe*, which connotes a group with free-flowing discussion. (*Quassel* means "to ramble," and *Strippe* means "string.")

Here, in these *Quasselstrippe*, a discerning observer could watch a new school of thought emerging. It would eventually be called *field theory*. To common parlance and to professional psychology it would contribute such words and concepts as *group dynamics, level of aspiration, cognitive structure,* and *action research.* During the next five decades, men and women tutored at these *Quasselstrippe* would conduct the most significant social psychological research on the phenomena of everyday experience. For the first time, armchair speculation and simple descriptive analysis would be set aside, and controlled experiments would take their place as the major tools for investigating such issues as leadership style, group cohesiveness, individual and organizational change, group decision making, cooperation and competition, and intergroup conflict.[3]

Lewin asserted that these issues were respectable, even essential, areas of concern for scientific psychology. He said this at a time when the other dominant schools of thought in psychology, such as associationism in Germany and behaviorism in the United States, had labeled these phenomena and others (such as intention, will, hope, and aspiration) as *verboten* and irrelevant. Their model of man can be likened to a machine whose sensory receptors passively receive stimuli and emit appropriately signaled responses. Lewin disagreed. He believed that men actively participate in organizing their environment and in responding to it. Human behavior, he said, is a product of the interaction of a person trying to cope with the environment as it is currently being experienced.[4] It is not a mechanistic by-product of conditioning through rewards and punishments, nor is it a mindless response to the irresistible urge of instinctual drives.

In their most basic form, Lewin's ideas are related to a common assumption of other dynamic theories in psychology. Such theories assert that human beings and other organisms strive to maintain an inner equilibrium. When they need or desire something, psychological tension is aroused and the desired equilibrium is disrupted. The successful attainment of appropriate goals restores equilibrium by lowering tension.

One day, in the Schwedishe Cafe, Lewin provided an important and amusing demonstration of this idea. The day was probably like most others. People assembled. Discussions started. Coffee and cake were ordered, and then ordered again and again as the hours passed. Someone finally called for the bill. *"Die Rechnung, bitte."* Despite the hours that had passed, the variety of items ordered, and the lack of a written record, the waiter provided a precise reckoning of the account. He knew just what each person had ordered and how much was owed. An insignificant display of a waiter's skills? Perhaps. But Lewin saw more in this everyday event. One-half hour later he called the waiter back and asked him to rewrite the check, accounting for each order as he had done before. The waiter was outraged. How could he possibly do that? They had already paid the bill. He could no longer remember.

Before they paid the bill, he was able to keep the tally in mind for hours. Thirty minutes after the bill was paid, it was gone. Lewin's demonstration was not scientifically precise, but it was a clever illustration of the way in which tension operates in everyday life. While the waiter's goal of having the bill paid was uncompleted, tension remained aroused. It caused him to think about relevant issues: the items which people had been ordering. Once the bill was paid, goal attainment was complete, and the tension was dissipated. The items could no longer be recalled.

Tension motivates action. It causes waiters to remember what they are owed and to collect the money they are due. If you want to go to a movie, tension creates psychological forces which cause appropriate goal-related activity. If you want to make love, it does the same. Until an appropriate goal, or some suitable substitute, is attained, tension keeps you aroused and active.[5]

During the decade following the event in the Schwedishe Cafe, Lewin and his students demonstrated time and again that human beings experience tension as a consequence of events in their own lives.[6] Recently, however, there was an even more profound discovery; researchers learned that human beings have the capacity to experience tension because of *another person's* experiences.[7]

Scientists often discover what it is already known, and both movie-goers and motion picture directors have known of this capacity for decades. Erotic episodes in films frequently heighten an audience's state of sexual arousal. The best of them are composed with a finesse that seduces onlookers into identifying with one of the characters. During the episode, and for a time after it ends, people imagine themselves in the role of one of the characters, being loved and touched and excited. Then all the juices start running, almost as if the experience were really one's own.

Empathic and vicarious transactions of this sort are not limited to sex. There is definite evidence that bystanders are aroused by the experiences of their fellows who are in distress. Measures of physiological and psychological reactions bear this out: hearts beat faster, perspiration increases, and blood pressure changes. People report being tense, nervous, and concerned. What is more, these responses become more extreme as the other's plight worsens[8] and when people believe that they and the other are *we*.[9]

One important bit of evidence for this assertion can be found in an experiment conducted as part of a Harvard doctoral dissertation prepared by Dennis Krebs,[10] who also wrote the most comprehensive review of psychological research on altruism and helping.[11](Published in 1970, the review is still an excellent source of information and ideas.)

People in Kreb's experiment watched another person receive either a reward (money) or a punishment (electric shock). They were not aware that this event was staged and the other person was helping the experimenter. Before the observation began, some of the people, selected at random, were led to believe that they were going to watch a person who was similar to them. Of course, this was also a hoax, perpetrated for experimental purposes. But everyone believed it, and there was no opportunity to check its validity. They just watched as the other was supposedly rewarded or punished. As they watched, their physiological reactions (heart rate, blood pulse volume, and skin resistance) were recorded. Changes in these reactions were greatest for those who believed that the other was *similar* to them. These people reported feeling most empathic, and they were also *most altruistic* when given the opportunity to help.

The feeling of similarity produced a bond. Through it, some people in Kreb's experiment were able to "exchange" places with the other and his experiences became their own. As Adam Smith said, ". . . it is by changing places in fancy with the sufferer that we come either to conceive or to be affected by what he feels."[12] What Adam Smith did not realize is that people do not indiscriminately change places with sufferers; they favor those to whom they can say "You and I are *we*." Whenever this occurs, ties exist creating the oneness which provides a basis for the arousal of what I shall call *promotive tension*. Bound together through a sense of identity, each person's plight is a concern for all. When one of their fellows needs aid, *we*-group members are not apathetic bystanders. They experience promotive tension, and being simultaneously hedonistic and unselfish, they seek to lessen this tension by acting on the other's behalf.

Because of the reputation that New Yorkers have, a few readers may be surprised to learn that some of the most convincing evidence of this human capacity for experiencing promotive tension and behaving selflessly comes from thousands of unsuspecting pedestrians on the streets of New York City's largest borough.

Notes

1. Much of the material that describes Lewin's personal history is drawn from Alfred J. Marrow's biography of Kurt Lewin, *The Practical Theorist* (New York: Basic Books, Inc., Publishers, 1969). Marrow was Lewin's friend and colleague from 1933, when Lewin first arrived in the United States, until his death in 1948.

2. A statement reported by Marrow in his biography of Lewin.

3. Most of this research is summarized by Morton Deutsch, "Field Theory in Social Psychology," in Gardner Lindzey and Elliot Aronson, *The Handbook of Social Psychology*, Volume I (Reading Mass.: Addison Wesley, 1969).

4. Kurt Lewin, *A Dynamic Theory of Personality* (New York: McGraw-Hill Book Company, 1935) and Kurt Lewin, *Principles of Topological Psychology* (New York: McGraw-Hill Book Company, 1936).

5. See Lewin, *A Dynamic Theory*, Chapter 1.

6. Bluma Zeigarnik, "Über das Behalten von Erledigten und Unerledigten Handlungen," *Psychologische Forschung*, 9 (1927), 1–85; Maria Ovsiankina, "Die Wiederaufnahme von Unterbrochenen Handlungen," *Psychologische Forschung*, 11 (1928), 302–79; H. B. Lewis, "An Experimental Study of the Role of the Ego in Work: I. The Role of the Ego in Cooperative Work," *Journal of Experimental Psychology*, 34 (1944), 113–26; H. B. Lewis and M. B. Franklin, "An Experimental Study of the Role of the Ego in

Work: II. The Significance of Task Orientation in Work," *Journal of Experimental Psychology*, 34 (1944), 195–215.

7. H. A. Hornstein, H. N. Masor, K. Sole, and M. Heilman, "Effects of Sentiment and Completion of a Helping Act on Observer Helping: A Case for Socially Mediated Zeigarnik Effects," *Journal of Personality and Social Psychology*, 17, no. 1 (1971), 107–12; Dennis L. Krebs, "Empathically Produced Affect and Altruism" (unpublished doctoral thesis, Harvard University, 1970).

8. R. S. Lazarus, E. M. Opton, M. S. Nomikos, and N. O. Rankin, "The Principle of Short-circuiting of Threat: Further Evidence," *Journal of Personality*, 33 (1965), 622–35.

9. D. Krebs, "Empathically Produced"; E. Stotland, "Exploratory Investigations of Empathy," in Leonard Berkowitz, ed., *Advances in Experimental Social Psychology, Volume IV* (New York: Academic Press, Inc. 1969).

10. Krebs, "Empathically Produced."

11. D. L. Krebs, "Altruism—an Examination of the Concept and a Review of the Literature," *Psychological Bulletin*, 73 (1970), 258–302.

12. Adam Smith, "The Theory of Moral Sentiments" (1759), in Herbert Schneider, ed., *Adam Smith's Moral and Political Philosophy* (New York: Hafner Publishing Co., Inc. 1948).

7

Promotive tension:
a tree grows in Brooklyn

What comes to mind when I say, " 'The Bums,' Ebbet's Field, Coney Island, Prospect Park, and Flatbush Avenue"? "Brooklyn" is the only right answer. Brooklyn, home of Nathan's hot dogs and knishes from Shatzkin's and Mrs. Stahl's. Brooklyn, site of Sheepshead Bay, 1950s rock-and-roll shows at the Brooklyn Paramount, and a bridge that was allegedly sold on repeated occasions to unwary out-of-towners. I grew up in Brooklyn, and in the spring of 1970, I returned there in order to learn why human beings help one another.[1]

What happened to the Brooklynites who unknowingly became involved in this investigation might happen to anyone. Imagine yourself walking along a street in some busy shopping area. It's spring, late afternoon, and the streets are filled with hustle-bustle; there are homeward-bound workers, slow-moving shoppers, and exploding children, freed from the special burden of attending school in the springtime. Odors from fruit markets, groceries, shoe stores, barbershops, delicatessens, and McDonald's all manage to blend in appetizing harmony. Perhaps you stop for some fattening delicacy, and then continue on your way. Suddenly, lying on the ground in front of you is a pair of envelopes paperclipped together. Protruding from one is a money order. You stoop down and pick them up.[2] Both envelopes are properly addressed and have postage affixed.

Inside, one contains a contribution to an organization (a two-dollar money order which is valueless to you), and the other contains a response to a public opinion poll questionnaire. There is no return address and all that you know about the sender is his or her initials, "B.G.W."

If you ask someone, "What would you do in these circumstances?" you will probably hear, "Why, I'd seal the envelopes and mail them." But, in reality, this does not always happen. Frequently, these lost letters are simply discarded. But that is very *unlikely* to occur when people are able to say of a stranger who needs their aid, "You and I are *we*." This is what Krebs found. A stranger's plight produced more extreme physiological arousal when he was similar; when there were bonds of *we*.

In Brooklyn, during the spring of 1970, *we*-group and *they*-group identity were established by changing the stranger's response to the public opinion poll question, which was "How do you feel about the current U.S. position on aid to Israel?" Some Brooklynites learned that the stranger was pro-Israeli. He said, "I feel that the U.S. should continue to provide aid to Israel to guarantee its survival." Others learned that he was pro-Arab: "The U.S. should not send any aid to Israel since I think the Arabs are right." In the heavily Jewish section of Brooklyn where these letters were "lost" residents felt closer to a pro-Israeli stranger than to a pro-Arab one. In fact, one week before the letters were dropped, we proved this very thing by conducting a survey in the area. Pedestrians were shown the entire array of material (both envelopes with all their contents) and were asked to indicate their feelings about the stranger. The evidence was unequivocal: the pro-Israeli stranger was part of the *we*-group; the pro-Arab stranger was not.[3]

When they were tied to a stranger through the bonds of *we*, nearly nine out of ten people helped by forwarding the lost material; but when they were separated by the barrier of *they*, only half that number provided help.[4] When this same experiment was repeated more than one year later, with hundreds of other people, the very same pattern emerged. It was no accident. These human beings were not guided by rigid instinctual demands. Their behavior reflected an ability that is unique to their species: the ability to use abstract cues like politics, religion, and race to form real and imaginary groups, and to picture oneself and others as an insider or an outsider, as *we* or *they*. United through a sense of identity, a stranger's plight aroused tensions in finders. Although they may have been totally unaware of exactly why they were doing it, these finders helped. The rest turned their backs and refused to perform a simple gesture of concern and kindness.

Tension caused by another's distress is the key to explaining this behavior. Other evidence tells us that any alternative explanation seems unlikely. Lewin and his students found that tension mounts as a person moves closer and closer toward some appropriate goal. A quote in *Women's Wear Daily*[5] captures this concept. In an article on shoplifting, one knowledgeable respondent said, "Ten percent of those we apprehended resisted arrest. The closer they are to the door, the more they fight to get away. If you arrest them far from the door they give you less trouble."

The closer one is to an end-point that is desirable, the greater the tension and the more one struggles to get there. But, the closer one is to an end-point that is undesirable, the greater the tension and the more one struggles to get away. If the theory of promotive tension is correct, if human beings experience tension because of another's plight, then more tension should be experienced, and more concern and altruism exhibited, when the other is on the verge of success at the time help is needed.

A form attached to the lost contribution (fig. 1) indicated to any finder that it was either the second or ninth in a series of ten such contributions. When it was the ninth contribution, and a stranger

FIG. 1

The Institute for Research in Medicine
IBM Incorporated (address)

We are pleased to announce that the MASOR foundation has agreed to match each $20.00 contribution from a concerned individual with $100.00, provided these $20.00 contributions are received by (DATE: either 9 or 2 weeks after the form was being mailed) for this campaign. This means you now have an opportunity to make a significant contribution to research in the battle against dread diseases. Rather than ask you to send $20.00 all at once, we hope that it will be easier for you to send $2.00 per week for each of ten weeks. Please detach the contribution form and mail it with your payment.

. . . .

This is my (   ) contribution. Only (   )more contribution(s) to go before my $20.00 becomes $120.00 in the fight against dread disease.

was close to completing the final goal of ten contributions, nearly everyone helped. But when the stranger's goal was distant, and it was only the second contribution, very few finders helped.[6] One explanation of this behavior seems likely. Promotive tension, born of *we*-group ties, mounted as the stranger approached nearer and nearer to the final goal.

These facts are testimony to every man's and woman's capacity for experiencing tension coordinated to *another's* goals and well-being. Human beings do not selfishly turn away from others who need aid. Nor do they all help. There are no instincts to compel behavior along a single path without regard to social conditions. When "you" and "I" become "we," bonds exist which allow promotive tension arousal. Human beings do not stand idly by, saying "Ho-hum," when their fellows are in distress. Through the formation of *we*, self-interest is fused together with a concern for others, and the basis of promotive tension and selfless behavior is born.

Preventive Helping: An Example of Human Perversity

One of life's frustrating realities is that loved ones, friends, and allies sometimes seek goals which we ourselves dislike. What happens then? How do human beings ordinarily respond if they have an opportunity to help someone they like attain a goal which they themselves dislike. Do the bonds of *we* cause helping regardless of another's goals? The answer is "No." If human beings disapprove of another's goals, promotive tension mounts as the other, identified as *we*, moves closer toward its attainment. But the rising tension does not produce the kind of helping that it did in Brooklyn. Acting as if they themselves were being drawn toward the undesirable end, people frequently seem immune to the other's desire and, instead of providing assistance, they act to *block* forward progress.

Tommy Smothers, the entertainer, captures the social and psychological relevance of this event in a song about helping which is included in a record album for children entitled, "Free to Be... You and Me." Two kinds of helping are identified in the song. One kind moves us closer to some desired end and, as Tommy Smothers sings, that help is what "helping is all about." The other kind is different. It prevents fulfillment of our desires and frequently causes us to think about the help-giver and moan, "with friends like these who needs enemies?" Poignantly the lyrics conclude that this sort of help "we can . . . do without."

Parents frequently provide their children with this second form of help. "It's for your own good," they say. Despite a youngster's earnest desire to plunge his fingers into an electric socket, join a teenage social club called the *Snarling Snakes*, or marry his "one and only," when loving parents consider the goal to be an undesirable one, they frequently act to prevent its attainment. This *preventive helping* occurs with greatest predictability when others are right on the verge of satisfying their desires.[7]

Once, hundreds of New Yorkers learned that a stranger was contributing to the *International Nudist Foundation*, a fictitious organization, which previously collected survey data indicated was intensely disliked by community residents. By changing the goal polarity from positive (the International Tuberculosis Foundation) to negative, we reversed the previously obtained pattern of helping. Evidence of that most perverse phenomenon, *preventive helping*, was strikingly clear. When a *liked* stranger was *close* to attaining a disapproved goal, only thirty-seven percent of the finders helped, but when he was relatively *more distant*, nearly sixty percent helped.[8]

So it is that on some occasions we "hurt the one we love." Rather than aid a fellow *we*-grouper's advance toward a disapproved goal, we act to block progress. And, in extreme circumstances, when the other is really close to achieving that which we deem unacceptable, we engage in *preventive helping* which, from the helper's viewpoint, is not the kind of help that helping is all about.

But make no mistakes, this perverse behavior is caused by the very same tension that causes true, unselfish behavior. Remember when your parents said, "I'm doing this because I love you"? They were right. Like other people, they were experiencing promotive tension, aroused by you, someone with whom they felt united as *we*, and they were acting to lessen this tension by moving you away from a goal which you desired, but they disliked. Their most unpleasant demands, however misguided, were very likely caused by the bonds of *we*, not the barrier of *they*.

Paradoxically, when a disliked goal is involved, someone who is a *we* is treated almost like someone who is a *they*. Which is probably close to what you recognized about your parents' behavior. Perhaps you can recall thinking, or being "naughty" enough to shout, "You don't love me"; "I might as well be a stranger around here"; or "I get more sympathy from my friends (or my friends' parents) than I get from you." Actually, they did not deserve such accusations because you were probably not being treated quite as badly as an outsider. In fact, from these investigations, I can tell you that when *they* are pursuing disapproved goals, helping is at a minimum. *They* received almost no help at all. Close to the goal a pitiful 27 percent received aid, and when *they* were distant from it only 31 percent received aid. On the average, this is nearly 20 percent less helping than *we*'s received when pursuing the same disapproved goal. No matter what the goal, *we*'s are helped more than *they!*

When You *and* I *Are* We

Dennis Krebs's investigation, which was described in the last chapter, is certainly the most distinct demonstration of the relationship between another's dilemma, one's own physiological and psychological response, and helping. But his findings are not isolated events. There is other research which also demonstrates a human being's capacity to be emotionally and physically aroused when his fellows are in distress. One very ambitious series of experiments has been conducted by Professor Ezra Stotland and his students.[9] Their work is too extensive to report in detail. Basically, the people in Professor Stotland's studies were in the same situation as were those in Krebs's. They observed someone, in reality Professor Stotland's confederate, having an unpleasant experience. At various times, this unfortunate fellow failed on a task, received electric shock, and experienced "painful" heat from a diathermy machine. Prior to this tragic episode, which was a sham, they were led to believe that the other was similar or dissimilar to them. This was accomplished in different ways. In one instance, for example, these people were permitted to compare their scores on a personality test with the other person's scores. Of course, both sets of scores were secretly falsified to produce feelings of similarity or dissimilarity.

The trends evident in Stotland's findings support what I have been saying: when people believed that the other fellow was similar to them, physiological reactions such as vasoconstriction and palmar sweating were most extreme. They also reported feeling more tense, nervous, and distressed.[10]

These results should come as no surprise. Most people who read novels, go to the movies, or watch T.V. shows have had similar experiences. Think about it. Surely you can remember occasions when you have identified with some hero or heroine. Perhaps you cried when their loved ones died, or stiffened as some hideous monster (human or otherwise) crept toward them. Or maybe you shouted with relief when they finally destroyed an archenemy who tormented them throughout the entire story. Film-makers and authors understand this basic and essential human capacity to be aroused by another's experiences, and they are careful to create characters with whom you, the observer, will identify. Sitting there, in the darkened theater, you are not simply someone who has paid an exorbitant price to watch a motion picture. For a little while, you are not *I*, isolated and alone. A kind of ego-extension occurs. *I* becomes part of a *we* and you are aroused by the pains and pleasures of other human beings.

These events are commonplace and familiar. They are part of the reason that movies and novels are fun. And they are profound examples of a human being's capacity to be aroused by the experiences of another human being. But they may not be uniquely human. Rats, monkeys, and other subhuman species exhibit similar behavior. They too seem to be aroused when witnessing the plight of a brother rat or monkey.

Consider an experiment by R. M. Church which appeared in the *Journal of Comparative and Physiological Psychology*.[11] Thirty-two rats that had reached the ripe old age of one-hundred days aided Church in this experiment. They were placed in a rather modern box with a lucite and stainless steel decor. Otherwise, this small cubicle's generally unadorned quality was disrupted only by a small lever which, over the course of several days, the rats learned to press in order to receive food. This happy life, which required only a simple response in order to receive a small, but from a hungry rat's viewpoint, delectable food pellet, lasted sixteen days. By that time the lever-pressing response was well learned. Then, suddenly, another rat was added to this tranquil scene. This little fellow was in an adjoining cage, exhibiting great distress and fear because it was receiving electric shock. This situation reduced bar-pressing to zero. The rats' previous behavior pattern, which provided them with tasty tidbits, was briefly disrupted when they witnessed brother rat being shocked. What is more, a rat's familiarity with electric shock made a difference. Those which were familiar with shock, and therefore had a basis for "empathizing," reacted strongly with depressed rates of bar-pressing.

Monkeys do the same thing. At times, they behave in ways that protect other monkeys from electric shock.[12] But their aid to fellow monkeys is not indiscriminate. Monkeys are often most likely to help other monkeys when the other is a cagemate (a monkey *we*-group?) and when they themselves are familiar with electric shock.

These studies with subhuman species are not uncontroversial. Nonethless, let us cautiously accept the idea that subhumans *may* become aroused when their fellows are in distress, while human beings *certainly do become so aroused.* Because members of our species are able to distinguish between *we* and *they,* and because our consciousness potentially includes the experience of being united with other human beings, we are sometimes compelled, for the sake of self-comfort, to act on another's behalf. Hedonism compels altruism!

But when is it that people are *we?* What are the ties that bind? In social life few questions are as important as these. Without these ties, human beings do not experience tension coordinated to the plight of their fellows. Without these ties, apathy, not activity, is the response to another's distress.

There is a Yiddish saying, "What the eyes don't see, the heart won't feel." When a *we*-group member is in trouble, it is as if one's eyes cannot be averted. They see, and truly *the heart feels.* But human beings are not always able to say, "You and I are *we.*" Sometimes others are *they.* Then, eyes do not see, hearts do not feel, and *their* trouble is not *my* concern. In order to create a society in which people are socially responsible and concerned about one another's welfare, above all else we must understand the ties that bind.

Notes

1. H. A. Hornstein, H. N. Masor, K. Sole, M. Heilman, "Effects of Sentiment and Completion of a Helping Act on Observer Helping: A Case for Socially Mediated Zeigarnik Effects," *Journal of Personality and Social Psychology,* 17, no. 1, (1971), 107–12.

2. People's willingness to retrieve this material is truly astounding. If the letters are placed in the center of an unlittered street, they are usually picked up by the first person to see them.

3. Liking for B.G.W. was indicated on a nine-point rating scale, labeled "would dislike B.G.W. very much" and "would like B.G.W. very much" at the extremes. The procedure used in the survey guaranteed

anonymity. The average ratings obtained for a pro- and anti-Israel B.G.W. were 7.60 and 3.00, respectively. There is less than one in a thousand chances that a difference this large could occur by chance. The survey also included a group of people who rated B.G.W. without knowing his view on Israel. All this group saw was his contribution form. They indicated a liking nearly as great as the one provided by the pro-Israel group. Using this group as a baseline, we can suppose that the pro-Israel information strengthened *we*-group ties only slightly, but pro-Arab information weakened them dramatically.

4. Approximately thirty people were originally included in each of the groups. The difference in the rate of return between these groups had less than a one out of twenty possibility of occurring by chance.

5. *Women's Wear Daily*, March 19, 1973.

6. The probability that these differences occurred by chance is less than one out of twenty.

7. At times, parents certainly try to "nip things in the bud." This occurs when the intended goal is intensely disliked, in which case any movement toward the goal is too much.

8. S. A. Hodgson, H. A. Hornstein, and E. LaKind, "Socially Mediated Zeigarnik Effects as a Function of Sentiment, Valance, and Desire for Goal Attainment," *Journal of Experimental Social Psychology*, 8 (1972), 446–56. Other parts of this experiment, which in no way provided evidence to alter the discussion in this book, can be found in the original source. In brief, these other components demonstrated that the other's evaluation of the goal had no effect on whether the goal was positive or negative. One's own evaluation of the other's goal was all that counted. One hundred and twenty found the Tuberculosis Foundation material, and an equal number found the Nudist Foundation packet. This difference is so large that there is only one chance out of one thousand that it occurred by chance.

9. Ezra Stotland, "Exploratory Investigations of Empathy," in Leonard Berkowitz, ed., *Advances in Experimental Social Psychology, Volume IV* (New York: Academic Press, Inc., 1969).

10. Stotland, Ibid., p. 272.

11. E. M. Church, "Emotional Reactions of Rats to the Pain of Others," *Journal of Comparative and Physiological Psychology*, 52 (1959), 132–34.

12. J. H. Masserman, S. Wechkin, and W. Terris, Jr., "Altruistic Behavior in Rhesus Monkeys," *American Journal of Psychiatry*, 121 (1964), 584–85; W. Wechkin, J. H. Masserman, and W. Terris, Jr., "Shock to a Conspecific as an Aversive Stimulus," *Psychonomic Science*, 1, (1964), 47–48.

8

Ties that bind

Time and circumstance inevitably change each human being's conception of who is *we* and who is *they*. Like slowly shifting sands, that which is important and critical in defining *we* is altered as both planned and uncontrollable events force us to one place, then another. A national famine will create one set of *we*-group boundaries, probably very restrictive ones. A national enemy will create a different set of boundaries, probably broad ones, encompassing all those with whom we are allied. As a lonely traveler in a foreign land, I may meet another countryman who speaks my language. Suddenly, almost everything else about my fellow traveler fades as the two of us become *we*, bound together as strangers in a strange land.[1]

But some things do not change. There are parts of each of us that remain constant despite life's vicissitudes. Often, perhaps too often, we use these parts to categorize ourselves and others into *we* and *they*. Our parents, neighborhood, race, religion, and nation are bestowed without prior discusson or approval. In time, we become partisan in our feelings toward these groups, favoring fellow members over anyone who is a *they*. When I was a boy, living on Argyle Road in Brooklyn, my friends and I *knew* that *we* were better than the Westminsters, who lived around the corner. No sacrifice on behalf of fellow "Argyles" was too great. This situation lasted for several years until we were suddenly struck with an insight: the

"Westminsters" were as good as we, and in every way, both of us were considerably better than the dullards from Coney Island Avenue a few blocks away.

Surely you can think of groups and situations that produced similar feelings in you—instances in which partisan feelings developed simply because you were part of a social situation that was familiar, safe, and comfortable. Frequently, without any more reason than this, the world is divided into *we* and *they*.

There are the few who avoid this process. Remaining open-minded, they distrust labels, social categories, and sweeping generalizations. They are exceedingly conscious of each human being's uniqueness and complexity, which they extol. For these people *we-they* boundaries do not exist; any other person's plight arouses promotive tension in them and becomes their concern. But few of us are so saintly. Knowing that we are a member of a group and another is not is usually sufficient to produce *we-they* distinctions.

Who Are We?

Three thousand people, in three cities, Boston, Paris, and Athens, produced an abundance of evidence supporting this conclusion. These people participated in five extremely creative investigations conducted by Roy Feldman.[2] In each of his investigations the general situation was the same: a native of the city was in a position to aid a stranger who was either a fellow countryman or a foreigner, a *we* or a *they*. Nothing more was known. In one investigation an unsuspecting native was asked for street directions. "Excuse me, sir," said Dr. Feldman or one of his associates (speaking in the appropriate language). "How do I get to Copley Square" (Boston), "La Place des Ternes" (Paris), or "Plateia Kyriakou" (Athens)? In a second investigation, natives were approached at either the Washington Street M.T.A. station (Boston), the Chausee D'Antin or Havre Caumartin underground stations (Paris), or the Omonia Square metro station (Athens). "Excuse me, sir, I'm waiting for someone here. Could you please mail this letter for me?" Honesty was tested in a third investigation when pedestrians were asked if they were the ones who had dropped a one dollar bill, or the local equivalent. Dr. Feldman wondered, whether they would be more likely to lie ("Yes. That's my money.") when the inquiry was made by a countryman or by a foreigner. Honesty was also tested in a fourth investigation when cashiers in pastry shops were deliberately overpaid, which gave them an opportunity to return the excess or keep it. The fifth investigation was the most daring of all. Feldman and his associates checked to see when it is that taxi drivers take the most direct route to a destination.

Many interesting findings were obtained during the course of these investigations. For example, Parisian taxi drivers were more dishonest with foreigners than any other group of cabbies. Although, I hasten to add, in defense of Paris, that in most of the other situations, Parisians treated Americans better than Americans treated foreigners. Beyond all these separate tidbits, there is one key point: Feldman summarizes his findings by saying, "In general, when a difference was observed, the Athenians treated a foreigner better than a compatriot, but Parisians and Bostonians treated compatriots better than foreigners."[3] Does this mean that Parisians and Bostonians abide by our proposition but Athenians do not? Do Athenians help *they*'s more than *we*'s, while everyone else helps *we*'s more than *they*'s?

No, not at all! In fact, the data provide a very neat confirmation of our proposition that *we* are helped, *they* are not. What of the Athenian behavior? you are wondering. Well, as Feldman mentions, it turns out that these findings are quite consistent with what we know of Athenians from independent scientific investigations conducted by Drs. Triandis, Vassiliou, and Nassiakou.[4] After examining the ingroup-outgroup concepts of Greeks, this team concluded that the Greek ingroup includes family, friends, friends of friends, and *tourists. Other Greeks are outgroup and* they. Greeks too prefer helping *we* more than *they*.

The ability to form *we-they* distinctions is very probably not a characteristic which is unique to human beings. An amazing variety of subhuman species seem to possess the capacity to form special ties with selected others. "Bonding"[5] is a most extreme form of this behavior. Involving a mutual attachment between two members of a species, it is a personal relationship which transcends a given time and place. Animals quite low on the phylogenetic scale exhibit this behavior, including various fish. Of course, as any zoo-goer or jungle-movie enthusiast knows, chimpanzees, canines, baboons, various felines, birds, and bovines all form into various sized groups. Members of these groups sometimes have special ties to one another which are exhibited through behavior reserved for ingroup members only. Once the group exists the capacity to be distressed about another group member's plight is not absent. Konrad Lorenz[6] writes in almost heartrending prose about how greylag geese mourn a dying group member. (Since I do not share Lorenz's affection for these biped, my account will be more matter-of-fact. To goose lovers, I apologize.) With outstretched wings, they stand over their moribund fellow goose, hissing. This sight of a goose keening its lost brethren, as sorrowful as it may be, is hardly a match for the scene that one will witness upon encountering a goose who has lost its triumph-ceremony partner, another goose with whom the first has very special and enduring bonds. "The first response to the disappearance of the partner consists in the anxious attempt to find him again. The goose moves about restlessly by day and night, flying all distances and visiting all places where the partner might be found. . . . From the moment a goose realizes that the partner is missing, it loses all courage and flees even from the youngest and weakest geese." As the word spreads through the gaggle, ". . . the lonely goose rapidly sinks to the lowest step in the ranking order." Shy, reluctant to approach its feeding place, this poor, forlorn bird tends to become increasingly accident-prone.[7]

Chimps and monkeys also exhibit *we-they* distinctions and act on behalf of their fellows. On several occasions, for example, they have been observed trying to bind the wounds of other chimps and monkeys. Instead of fleeing, monkeys have even confronted their fiercest predators in order to save one of their fellows. Stories about cats and dogs who grow up together and ultimately defend each other against members of their own species are also familiar and abundant. But Konrad Lorenz exceeds all this anecdotal evidence when he tells the story of a Zurich zookeeper who was accidently injured by an elephant he had attended for some time. Injuries by elephants are nothing to be scoffed at, and no one in the vicinity was scoffing, neither the onlookers nor the elephant. Not realizing what had happened, but finding the familiar zookeeper in the cage, injured, the elephant did as it would do for any enfeebled member of its herd. It defended the zookeeper. So well, in fact, that others were unable to reach him with essential aid.

Unhappily, *we-they* distinctions do not simply lead to concern and aid for members of the *we*-group. There are times when *they* are discriminated against and treated rather harshly. In this regard, human beings and subhuman species share an unpleasant similarity: that which is strange and unfamiliar causes us to both recoil and attack. *The Painted Bird*, by Jerzy Kosinski,[8] is a morbid, tragic, and brilliantly written novel. Its title is taken from a vignette within the novel that has special significance for this discussion.

Jerzy Kosinski's main character is a small, dark-haired boy who wanders through Eastern Europe, going from one nightmarish experience to another. His journey begins at the outbreak of World War Two, which is a fitting backdrop for the demonic and inhumane behavior that surrounds this small lost child.

Early in his wanderings, the boy meets Lekh, who catches birds. These he exchanges for food and other necessities. For a time the boy aids Lekh in setting traps and caring for some of the birds which Lekh keeps. In the main, Lekh treated the boy well. From time to time, however, when he was depressed, Lekh did a strange thing. He took one of his captured birds and painted it, ". . . until it became more dappled and vivid than a bouquet of wildflowers." The boy and Lekh would then go into the forest. A small squeeze would cause the painted bird to cry out, attracting a flock of the same species. Around and around they would circle, until their painted brother, frenzied with desire to join them was released. But he never accomplished his goal. A simple coat of paint rendered him a *they*. It rested upon his feathers, a fradulent mark of Cain, for all to see. First the other birds recoiled, keeping the painted bird at a distance. Then they attacked and attacked until the painted bird fell, battered, with blood soaking its painted feathers.

Actually, Kosinski's fiction is accurate. Niko Tinbergen,[9] ethologist and Nobel Laureate, was part of an episode similar to the one that Lekh's depression precipitated. In order to conduct some studies of the herring gull, Tinbergen set a net trap. One gull, captured in this device was immediately attacked by his fellow gulls. Why should this happen? Only a moment before fate played an unfortunate trick on this fellow he had been one of the boys. One answer seems evident: the other herring gulls attacked their trapped companion because it was acting strangely; with uncharacteristic movements it was trying to extricate itself from Tinbergen's net trap! Stigmatized by his unusual, but unavoidable behavior, this gull became a *they*.

Xenophobia is a word which describes the way in which people respond to a *they*, someone who is different; it means a dislike of foreigners. Robert Ardrey, however controversial his ideas may be, does, undeniably, have a way with words. Speaking of xenophobia, Ardrey once wrote:

The howling monkey roars, alerting his fellows in the clan; the spider monkey barks; the lion without ceremony, attacks. However the animosity for strangers is expressed, whether through attack or avoidance, xenophobia is there, and it is as if throughout the animal world invisible curtains hang between the familiar and the strange.[10]

Through these curtains there are no bonds that allow arousal of promotive tension.

Michael Erwin, a fictitious character, once helped to provide some additional proof about xenophobic reactions and promotive tension. Michael Erwin, poor fellow, lost his wallet. (In fact, over a three-year period, he lost his wallet several hundred times.) But New York pedestrians near Union Square, Madison Square Park, or 34th Street (near Macy's) did *not* simply find Michael's wallet. What they found was an envelope from which Michael's wallet protruded, with a letter wrapped around it. The letter made it very clear to these unsuspecting pedestrians that they were not the wallet's first finder. Rather, they were its second finder. The first one was well-intended but ill-fated. He or she had prepared the envelope and the letter, and was in the process of returning the wallet with this material when the whole thing was lost. Since the wallet was attractive, and contained some money (two dollars), we wondered when people would complete the act of returning it to Michael Erwin, its rightful owner. An important determinant of when this actually occurred was the letter's contents.

In one case the previous finder said, "Dear Mr. Erwin, I found your wallet, which I am returning. Everything is here just as I found it." Sometimes he or she added, "I must say that it has been a great pleasure to be able to help somebody in the small things that make life nicer. It's really been no problem at all and I'm glad to be able to help." On other occasions, the previous finder identified himself or herself as a stranger, a foreigner to these shores; perhaps one of the people Emma Lazarus was asking for when she said, "Give me your tired, your poor, your huddled masses yearning to breathe free." This time the previous finder said, "Dear Mr. Erwin, I am visit your country finding your ways not familiar and strange. But I find your wallet which I here return. Everything is here just as I find it." And sometimes he or she added, "It great pleasure to help somebody with tiny things which make life nicer. It is not problem at all and I glad to be able to help." Nothing more was said.

When the first samaritan was *not* identified as a foreigner, two-thirds of the pedestrians helped by returning the wallet, but fewer than one-third helped when that first samaritan was a foreigner, a *they*. Michael Erwin, a hapless victim, suffered because this group of human beings was unmotivated to help a foreigner, a *they*, complete an act of mercy.[11]

Painted Birds Provoke No Pity

Once, thirty-two young boys who lived in the suburbs of Bristol, England, had an unusual experience. It began innocuously: Sitting together in groups of eight, they watched a cluster of dots flash on a screen. After seeing a cluster for only an instant, each of the Bristol boys had to guess the number of dots it contained. They did this time and again, until forty clusters passed before them. Their guesses were collected and examined with the care befitting a scientific experiment. Then, in privacy, four of the boys were each solemnly told, "You belong to a group of people who tend to *overestimate* the number of dots in a cluster"; and, with equal solemnity, the remaining four were each told, "You belong to a group of people who tend to *underestimate* the number of dots in a cluster."

Learning that one tends to over- or underestimate the number of dots in a cluster may not impress you as a particularly profound existential experience. I agree. But that is exactly what makes this event so important. These Bristol boys learned something about themselves that was absolutely trivial. What is more, the information was false; the labels "overestimator" and "underestimator" were assigned randomly and had nothing at all to do with anyone's actual performance. Nevertheless, despite their banality and irrelevance, these labels had dramatic effects on the Bristol boys' subsequent behavior.

After completing their encounter with the dots, each boy was individually escorted to a small room where an entirely new task was explained. This task required each boy to decide how to divide a sum of money between two of his fellows. Some promises were also made: first, that none of the other boys would ever know what he decided; second, that his own earnings would be unaffected by his decisions. For just a few moments, the Bristol boys were to be financial demigods, dispensing and withholding riches with impunity. Whatever they desired was possible: they could judiciously provide their fellows with approximately equal rewards, or they could favor one, causing the other to suffer losses.

Only one burr disrupted this otherwise smooth arrangement. They could not actually identify who would be affected by their decisions. One tiny bit of information was all that was supplied: they were given each boy's code number and from it they could determine whether he was an overestimator or an underestimator.

Most of us prefer to believe that if we had to make the kind of decision that faced these boys, this information would be irrelevant. Who cares whether someone tends to over- or underestimate the number of dots in a cluster? "The riches should be divided equally," we proclaim. But that turns out not to be what happens. In this experiment, and in many others using equally trivial distinctions, one consistent finding has emerged: people tend to discriminate in favor of others who are similar and against those who are dissimilar. Another human being's habit in judging dots becomes the spot of paint that renders him a *they*.[12]

Henri Tajfel, a garrulous, charming, and provocative professor of social psychology at the University of Bristol, was the principal creator of these experiments. Eventually he used the data to support a rather important claim, one which is directly relevant to our consideration of when people are likely to say, "You and I are *we*." Tajfel argued that people use any available criteria, however trivial, in order to organize their world into *we* and *they*, ingroups and outgroups. As we have seen, merely knowing that one person belongs to a group in which you also hold membership and another does not is often sufficient to produce action on behalf of the *we*-group member. Think about it: this happened in Brooklyn as well as in Bristol.

Brooklynites knew one thing about a stranger: his or her opinion on the Middle-East crisis. This was the only information available, and it was the salient dimension for determining *we*- or *they*-group membership. The stranger could have been a Democrat, a housewife, a laborer, or a war hero. But, in that one instant, all these possibilities were irrelevant. Once they learned that the stranger was pro-Arab, Brooklynites in our investigations could not say "You and I are *we*." A barrier was momentarily created, and through it there were no bonds which would allow the arousal of promotive tension. The stranger's plight was not their concern.

Bristol and Brooklyn are separated by more than three thousand miles, but data gathered at both places show how easily *we*- and *they*-groups are formed; and, once formed, how dramatically they affect behavior toward others. But there are aspects of these experiments which are troublesome. The Bristol boys and Brooklynites had only one bit of information about some other person. They knew either another Bristol boy's habit in estimating dots, or a stranger's view about the Middle-East crisis. This is not reality. Rarely do we know only one thing about some other person. Even when our only knowledge of another is his or her appearance, we are able to make a number of inferences about income, education, strength, and attractiveness to other males and females. We can judge their concern with cleanliness and their taste in clothing. Under ordinary circumstances, information about another person is plentiful. Unfortunately, it is also often contradictory, forcing us to recognize that we are similar in some ways, but different in others. What happens then? How and when are *we*-groups formed when lots of information is available, only some of which suggests similarity? Do human beings work like adding machines, subtracting each dissimilarity from each similarity, in order to determine which is predominant? Or are there times when a single dissimilarity is sufficient to cast a stranger out of *we* and into *they*?

Data gathered from more than one thousand unsuspecting pedestrians indicate that when human beings are faced with the question of whether they should help a stranger, they do *not* act like adding machines. Yet they are harsh judges. A single dissimilarity can cause them to label a stranger as *they*.[13]

In one experiment, pedestrians found a two-dollar contribution to a fictitious organization of which neighborhood residents told us they heartily approved, and a completed response to the Harcourt Public Opinion Service's monthly questionnaire. But, this time, the stranger, our fictitious victim, gave his opinion on *four* issues, not just one.[14]

From an earlier survey of the area we knew that neighborhood residents' opinions about the statements were almost unanimous, and we also knew that people in the neighborhood agreed that the issues were so important that, if they knew another person's opinion, yea or nay, it would have a dramatic effect on their judgment of that person.[15]

Because four statements were used we were able to vary the degree of agreement between a finder and a stranger who needed help. Some finders met a stranger who exhibited 100 percent agreement with their opinions. Others met one who either agreed with their opinions on three of the four statements (75 percent), two of the four statements (50 percent), one of the four (25 percent), or none of the four (0 percent).[16] Of course we could not be exactly certain about any one finder's views, but because our poll said that community opinion was nearly unanimous, the odds that finders held these views of the stranger were decidedly in our favor.

Nearly 70 percent of the finders helped when the stranger's opinions were in 100 percent agreement with their own, but with anything less than total agreement, an average of only 44 percent of the finders helped.[17] A single dissimilarity ripped the bonds of *we* asunder. Human beings do not readily experience tension because of another's distress, when all they can say to that other is, "*Sometimes* you and I are *we*." Insofar as *we*-group bonds and promotive tension arousal are concerned, either you are *we* or you are *they;* either you are *in,* or you are *out;* and if you are out, a miss is as good as a mile. *When important issues are involved, even a slightly painted bird provokes no pity.*

As a matter of fact, for the bonds of *we* to be shattered, the dissimilarity does not even have to be an important one. Tajfel proved that. Human beings will use whatever information they can to identify whether another human being is *we* or *they.*

When we repeated the experiment with hundreds of other people, this time using absolutely trivial statements like "All sports events should be broadcast on television two times," roughly the same picture emerged.[18]

Finding trivia was more difficult than we anticipated. Some people seem willing to regard almost any issue as important, which is, unhappily, one reason why people so continuously create *we-they* distinctions. Several hundred neighborhood residents had to be polled until we found four statements which were so *unimportant* that neighborhood residents almost unanimously agreed that if they knew another person's opinion, yea or nay, it would have no effect on the judgment of that other person.[19]

This time, when opinion similarity was total, only 51 percent of the people helped the stranger. When it was partial, the number of helpers dropped still further, to between 30 and 38 percent. And when there was no opinion similarity whatsoever, a token group of only 19 percent helped the stranger. Once again there is evidence that human beings are not machines, indiscriminately adding and subtracting similarities and dissimilarities. But human beings are not totally insensitive to the importance of similarities and dissimilarities. The overall level of helping was much lower than before. Agreement about trivia *does not* readily produce feelings of oneness.

We-group formation and helping are both curtailed when people's only bond with their fellows is shared membership in a social grouping which they regard as unimportant.

One other observation: unlike the previous investigation, in which important issues were involved, complete disagreement about trivial matters seems to have had particularly harmful effects. Only 19 percent of that group of finders bothered to forward the lost contribution. One can almost hear people saying, "If we can't agree about issues like these, then we certainly can't agree on any important ones. Stranger, whoever you are, you are certainly a *they!*" It seems that help is not readily dispensed to those who share our beliefs in the unimportant and commonplace, but it is actively withheld from those who consistently refute these beliefs.

Some We's Can Be They's

In scientific research, each time a question is answered, new lights and new shadows are created. Like all shadows, the new ones formed by our discoveries created images that teased and intrigued us. We wondered, "What would happen if finders encountered a stranger who was *we* along important dimensions and *they* along trivial ones?" Friends and kin regularly aid one another despite disagreements. Their *we*-group ties are not shattered because of minor dissimilarities. The bonds of their relationship are held secure by a recognition of unity in critical matters. In fact, there are times when friends[20] and kin[21] are so strong in their desire to maintain *we*-group ties that they misperceive each other's beliefs. Straining toward *we*, they build bonds out of false hope and illusion. But the principle underlying promotive-tension arousal applies nonetheless. It is blind to whether the bonds of *we* are rational or irrational, false or true. If one person can say to another, "You and I are *we*," then the effect will be the same: *we* are helped; *they* are not.

In one study, pedestrians found a stranger's lost contribution and the Harcourt Public Opinion form containing four statements, two important ones and two trivial ones. If finders agreed with a stranger's responses to *both* the important statements, then they were very likely to help by forwarding the lost material to its destination. Nothing else mattered.[22] These human beings were not likely to withhold aid from their fellows just because they disagreed about whether "All sports events should be broadcast on television two times" or whether there should be a charge for delivery of groceries. Disagreements about these matters faded into comparative irrelevance when they were set in a context of agreement about important matters. Agreement and disagreement about trivia is critical only when that is all there is to agree and disagree about.

Human beings are not thoughtless servants of instinct. Nor are they uncaring creatures. They examine surrounding social conditions and use whatever information is available to form judgments about another human being's identity as *we* or *they*. Physical appearances, attitudes, race, religion, political affiliations, habits in judging dots, and nationality, together and separately, are capable of influencing these judgments. Time and circumstance, not instinct, will determine their relative influence and potencies. Ultimately, the judgments themselves are the psychological substance that we use to erect or erode relationships. Human beings are caring and kind and helpful to one another only when they are united through a sense of identification. In the ordinary course of daily life, where experience with others involves both the important and the trivial, an *absence of dissimilarity in important matters* is essential if a human being is to see a stranger and say, "You and I are *we*."

Pseudospecies

Painted birds and herring gulls are obviously not the only ones who suffer because they are *they* through no fault of their own. Strangers sometimes "suffered" at the hands of Brooklynites because they happened not to share their opinions; Bristol boys "suffered" at the hands of other Bristol boys because their habit in estimating dots differed; and thousands of human beings living in Boston, Paris, and Athens, caused thousands of others to "suffer" because of differences in birthplace.

It was once believed that subhuman species had built-in inhibitions against seriously harming conspecifics. More recent evidence suggests that this is probably not the case,[23] although if a species is to survive, inflicting mortal harm on conspecifics cannot be a predominant mode of behavior. There is a sense in which human beings only rarely harm members of their own species, those for whom they experience *Zusammengehörigkeitsgefühl* (a feeling of belonging together), the *we*-group. That behavior is reserved for members of other species, perhaps better called pseudospecies, the *they*-

group. Man is the only creature on earth whose cognitive abilities allow him to organize the world along abstract dimensions such as religion, politics, and dot-judging traits. These dimensions, born of man's most advanced faculties, ironically allow human beings to harm other human beings because they are not classified as members of his species, but are rather part of another pseudospecies, the *they*-group.

We-groups, and their attendant compassion, empathy, and sympathy are all obstacles which prevent a human being from standing by idly as his fellows suffer. With morbidly bizarre insight, this fact was recognized by the Nazis. In order to pave the way for genocide, Rosenberg, Streicher, Goebbels and other Nazi propagandists set about developing racial distinctions to separate Jews, Gypsies, and East Europeans from Aryans. These non-Aryans were proclaimed *Untermenschen* (subhumans). An invisible curtain descended, a pseudospecies was created. Certainly, these others were not members of an Aryan's *we*-group. The Nazi success in creating this image will forever be a sorrowful testimony to the hazards of *we-they* distinctions.[24]

So it is that the same process which causes human beings to experience promotive tension, and act on each other's behalf, also provides the basis for human beings to destroy one another. The ties that bind us to some of our fellows, paradoxically, provide the foundation for helping them and destroying those with whom we are not bound. Separated from us by *we*-group barriers, *their* plight is not our concern. For *them* we experience no promotive tension. *We*-group ties, which are sometimes temporary and sometimes permanent, always seem to cause us to forget the Old Testament admonition, "You know the heart of the stranger, for you were strangers in the land of Egypt,. . . therefore love the stranger." The message has meaning for all human beings, for just as we are all *we*'s, we are also all *they*'s.

Notes

1. S. N. Hermon and E. O. Schild, "The Stranger-group in a Cross-cultural Situation," *Sociometry*, 24, no. 2 (1961), 165–76.
2. R. Feldman, "Response to a Compatriot and Foreigner Who Seek Assistance," in Leonard Bickman and Thomas Henchy, eds., *Beyond the*

Laboratory: Field Research in Social Psychology (New York: McGraw-Hill Book Company, 1972).

3. Feldman, Ibid. p. 53.

4. H. C. Triandis, V. Vassiliou, and M. Nassiakou, "Three Cross-cultural Studies of Subjective Culture," *Journal of Personality and Social Psychology Monograph Supplement*, 8, no. 4 (1968), part 2.

5. John Hurrell Crook, ed., *Social Behavior in Birds and Mammals: Essays on the Social Ethology of Animals and Man* (London: Academic Press, Inc., 1970); Konrad Lorenz, *On Aggression* (New York: Bantam Books, Inc., 1967); Anne Roe and George Gaylord Simpson, eds., *Behavior and Evolution* (New Haven: Yale University Press, 1958); M. R. A. Chance, "The Nature and Special Features of the Instinctive Social Bonds of Primates," in Sherwood L. Washburn, ed., *Social Life of Early Man* (Chicago: Aldine, 1961).

6. Lorenz, *On Aggression*.

7. Lorenz, Ibid, pp. 200–1.

8. Jerzy Kosinski, *The Painted Bird* (New York: Houghton Mifflin Company, 1965).

9. Niko Tinbergen, *The Herring Gull's World* (London: Collins, 1953).

10. Robert Ardrey, *The Social Contract* (New York: Dell Publishing Co., Inc., Delta Books, 1970), p. 269.

11. H. A. Hornstein, E. Fisch, and M. Holmes, "Influence of a Model's Feelings About His Behavior and His Relevance as a Comparison on Other Observers' Behavior," *Journal of Personality and Social Psychology*, 10, (1968), 222–26.

12. H. Tajfel, C. Flament, M. G. Billig, and R. P. Bundy, "Social Categorization and Intergroup Behavior," *European Journal of Social Psychology*, 1, no. 2 (1971), 149–78. Also, M. G. Billig, "Social Categorization and Intergroup Relations" (unpublished Ph.D. dissertation, University of Bristol, England, 1972.)

13. M. Deutsch, J. R. H. Thomas, and K. Garner, "Social Discrimination on the Basis of Category Membership" (mimeograph, Teachers College, Columbia University, 1971). Also, Mary Chase, "Categorization and Affective Arousal: Some Behavioral and Judgmental Consequences" (Unpublished doctoral dissertation, Teachers College, Columbia University, 1971).

14. K. Sole, J. Marton, and H. A. Hornstein, "Opinion Similarity, and Helping: Three Field Experiments Investigating the Bases of Promotive Tension," *Journal of Experimental Social Psychology*, 11, no. 1 (1975), 1–13.

15. In reality a third criterion was also employed. Respondents had to believe that only a moderate percentage of people in the neighborhood

shared their belief. This was, in fact, a misperception, since we had evidence of near unanimity; nevertheless, it eliminated the possibility that an individual who expressed a particular opinion would be seen by finders as a bizarre deviant.

16. The order in which the statements were presented and the order of agreement and disagreement were randomized for each finder so that none of the effects which we obtained can be attributed to accidents of format.

17. Use of proper statistical procedures indicates that there is very little likelihood that differences this large can be attributed to chance.

18. K. Sole, Marton, and Hornstein, "Opinion Similarity."

19. Once again, use of proper statistical procedures indicates that there is only a very small possibility that a difference this large could have occurred by chance.

20. Theodore Newcomb, *The Acquaintance Process* (New York: Holt, Rinehart & Winston, Inc., 1961).

21. D. Byrne and B. Blaylock, "Similarity and Assumed Similarity of Attitudes Between Husbands and Wives," *Journal of Abnormal and Social Psychology*, 67 (1963), 636–40.

22. Sole, Marton, and Hornstein, "Opinion Similarity." There is little likelihood that these differences could arise by chance.

23. Clarence R. Carpenter, *Naturalistic Behavior of Non-Human Primates* (Universitiy Park, Penn.: The Pennsylvania State University Press, 1964), for example, reports that infanticide frequently occurred as rhesus monkeys were being transported from India to the island of Santiago in Puerto Rico.

24. *Untermenschen* are also created by war comics (see N. Johnson, "What Do Children Learn from War Comics," *New Society*, July 7, 1966, pp. 7–12) and by juvenile delinquents, who frequently claim that their victims are homosexuals, bums, or other undesirable deviants (see G. M. Sykes and D. Matze "Techniques of Neutralization: A Theory of Delinquency," *American Sociological Review*, 22, (1957) 664–70.

9

Some news is good news

By June, 1968, "losing" wallets on mid- and lower-Manhattan streets was a comfortable habit. For several months my associates and I were "losing" them at an average rate of forty per day. In retrospect, it seems to me strange that such odd behavior could become so familiarly pleasant. But it did, and I have fond memories of our activities that spring. Weather permitting, each day we would assemble, carrying scores of wallets filled with small sums of money and sundry documents, all of which looked well used after a healthy churning in a clothes dryer. Ready with these, the tools of our trade, we traveled downtown by subway to Battery Park, Union Square, Madison Square Park, or 34th Street, near Macy's. Surreptitiously, the wallets were dropped to the ground, one by one, for unsuspecting passersby to retrieve.

By lunch time the day's quota was completed and we headed home in order to count the returns that were mailed to us by good samaritans who found our wallets on preceding days. On the average, about 45 percent of the people who found these wallets returned them. In fact, during all the months that we worked, only one major exception to the general pattern occurred: not a single one of the wallets lost on June 4, 1968, was returned. During the night a bullet fired by Sirhan Sirhan smashed through the skull of Robert F. Kennedy, killing him, and simultaneously eliminating whatever motives caused people to return our fictitious stranger's lost wallet.

I do not doubt that a few well-intentioned people were extremely upset by this event and were unable to return the wallets simply because they misplaced them. But this explanation seems to me insufficient to account for the widespread social irresponsibility that we observed. Indeed, there is empirical evidence that news of events such as Robert Kennedy's murder cause subconscious alterations in a person's conceptions of the moral-ethical commitments of the human community, and these changes ultimately create or destroy the social bonds which determine whether human beings are concerned about one another's welfare.

Individual conceptions about the *human community* are ill-founded generalizations which are shaped by information received about other people, in particular. It is as if all humankind were enclosed in a room which permits each of us to look at just some of them through an idiosyncratic collection of keyholes. Based on this keyhole sampling, we then proceed to make decisions about "human nature," which lies nestled inside us, secretly guiding our behavior toward others, until peeks through other keyholes provide new information.

One keyhole is our firsthand experience. Another is what people tell us. And a third, very critical one, is mass media news reporting. As I will demonstrate, this keyhole, like the others, prejudices ideas about other peoples' beliefs and values. News reports which symbolically portray "human goodness" cause inflated beliefs about the likelihood that people, in general, have moral-ethical commitments which concern them with others' well-being, including one's own. But those which portray "man's inhumanity" cause inflated beliefs about the likelihood that others have commitments antithetical to others' well-being, including one's own.

Thus, the news is *not* psychologically neutral. It is an important yet subtle source of influence on assumptions about others and behavior toward them. By changing one's general conception of people, news reports play a critical role in shaping specific inferences about strangers. They act as a bias, creating expectations which predispose us subconsciously to classify complete strangers as *we* or *they*.

Good News and Bad

Another Kennedy, the President of the United States, John F. Kennedy, was murdered on November 22, 1963. Not too many hours later, thirty men and women who were participating in a scientific investigation recorded their disillusionment with human nature and demonstrated how news events alter individual conceptions of the human community's moral-ethical disposition.

Lawrence S. Wrightsman and Frank C. Noble,[1] the investigators, found that in this group of thirty, the most unfavorable views of humanity's moral-ethical dispostion were endorsed by those people who liked President Kennedy and experienced a sense of personal loss because of his murder. Presumably this occurred because these people were more distressed by the events of November 22nd than the others who disliked the President and felt no personal grief when they heard of his assassination. But four months later, in March, 1964, the effects of that heinous crime dissipated. Grief and outrage surrendered to the ordinary pains and pleasures of daily living, and the same grief-ridden men and women who initially held comparatively unfavorable views of human nature were now considerably more positive in their outlook. As Wrightsman and Noble cautiously conclude, ". . . the effects of that November (22nd) weekend in Dallas did strongly, if temporarily, alter some persons' general attitudes toward human nature."[2]

Using far less extreme events than the murder of a charismatic national figure, my colleagues and I have uncovered additional evidence of the ways in which reports of good and bad news events alter individuals' conceptions of their community's values and beliefs, thereby affecting *we*-group ties. In one sense we have learned that the morning news may determine whether one human being will take the moment that is necessary in order to help another one who is in distress.

Forty-five men and twenty-two women sat by themselves waiting for a psychological investigation of human judgment and decision making to begin. They were college students in New York City who responded to newspaper ads in the hope of earning a little extra money. While they waited, music quietly sounded from a radio. The music was of the sort that one hears in a supermarket—unimaginative, unobtrusive, and unarousing. Minutes passed, the music ended, and there was a news report. "Here is a story in today's news," the announcer said in a trained professional tone. Some of the listeners then heard him add:

> A middle-aged man will be saved thanks to a person he has never met. The man, who suffers from a fatal kidney disease, had only a short while to live without an emergency kidney transplant. WWBG had broadcast pleas for help. Late last night a respected clergyman came to the hospital and offered to help. The donor has refused the family's offer to pay his hospital costs. Even in this day and age, some people hear a call for help.

But others, selected at random, heard:

> A seventy-two-year-old sculptress, beloved by neighborhood children for her statues of Winnie-the-Pooh, was strangled in her apartment last night by what appears to be a self-styled executioner. The murderer, who has been identified as a respected clergyman, was a long-time neighbor of the victim. He had the keys to the apartment because he occasionally babysat for the victim's grandchildren and was in the habit of bringing up her mail and packages.

The radio broadcast resumed its medley of nonmusic for a moment, then it was turned off by an experimenter, and the listeners, unaware that the news report was a hoax, were asked to guess the answers to several questions about the moral-ethical dispositions of people in general. For example, they were asked, "What percentage of people lead clean, decent lives?" "What percentage of people are basically honest?" "What percentage of people try to apply the Golden Rule even in today's complex society?" The percentage guesses that these men and women provided exhibited a pattern compatible with the one obtained by Wrightsman and Noble: after hearing bad news, people thought much less of their fellows. In contrast to those who heard good news, they estimated that fewer members of their community were honest, decent, and altruistic.[3] The essential details of this experiment were repeated on other occasions using considerably younger and older groups of males and females, and with news reports containing different contents.[4] On every occasion the same results occurred—good news produced more favorable views of humanity's moral-ethical disposition than bad news.

Julian Bond, a Georgia politician, wrote a poem in 1963 after President Kennedy's assassination:[5]

An old lady in the Delta
on hearing the news said
If they can do that to him
what won't they do to us

This poem captures feelings that nearly everyone has had at one time or another after hearing news of a horrendous misdeed. "Are we next?" "Who is responsible for this evil?" Uncertain about the answers to these questions, for a while we move about the world a little more fearfully, suspicious and concerned about "what they won't do to us." But who is "they"? "They" can't be everyone. Is my family "they"? My neighbors? What about the stranger, the one who sat near me on the bus, the one dressed so strangely, was he a "they"? Are you a *they? Who is a they?*

The observations that were made after the murders of John and Robert Kennedy, and those made after people heard our false news reports lead me to conclude that the boundaries of *they* grow larger after bad news and smaller after good news. It is as if good news creates a *love prejudice* and bad news a *hate prejudice.*[6] As is the case with all prejudices, these two color reality. A love prejudice predisposes us toward seeing our fellows as belonging to a moral-ethical community in which we share membership; one that is infused with beliefs and values which we endorse and one in which our personal well-being is a concern of other members. But a hate prejudice leads us to view our fellows as belonging to another moral-ethical community, one that is characterized by alien beliefs and values which are unmindful of or threatening to our personal well-being. Strangers about whom we have no information whatsoever are pressed by our prejudices into one or the other of these imagined groups, causing them to be joined with or separated from us by the bonds of *we* or the barriers of *they.* In this way, news of seemingly distant and unrelated events becomes an influence upon one's behavior toward total strangers.

Guilt or Innocence?

Elizabeth LaKind caused fifty middle-aged women, most of them housewives, to overhear a radio broadcast. Twenty-five of them heard good news, which prior inquiries indicated would create a favorable view of humanity. The remainder heard bad news, which prior inquiries indicated would produce an unfavorable view.[7] A brief period of music followed the broadcast, after which Ms. LaKind turned off the radio and asked the women to read summaries of two lawsuits. In the first a man was being accused of murder. In the second, another man was being sued for injuries sustained by a passenger in his car during an accident. Both cases had been previously examined by similar groups of women who had *not* listened to the news reports. They judged the two defendants as neither clearly innocent nor guilty. But after hearing the news reports, the judgments of these fifty women showed greater consensus. Those who heard *good news* were far more likely to judge the alleged murderer to be innocent than those who heard bad news. A similar trend was evident in the accident case.

These women all read exactly the same information. Indeed, they read the very same information that caused a similar group of women to be undecided about the defendants' innocence or guilt. Yet the twenty-five women who heard good news reports were more likely to be trusting and merciful than the ones who heard bad news reports. A radio description of events that occurred thousands of miles away, involving apparently unrelated people, altered their conceptions of the moral-ethical disposition of people, in general, and caused them to judge a hypothetical stranger as innocent or guilty of a crime.

Another psychologist, Dr. Alicia Singer, has observed very similar happenings.[8] In her research, Dr. Singer employed the services of men and women who were serving on jury duty. These people, who might have participated in an actual trial, listened to tape recordings of trials made from courtroom transcripts. Then, as if the trial were really occurring, they tried to reach a decision about the defendant's innocence or guilt. One day, an unexpected event, the Kent State massacre, interfered with the smooth flow of Dr. Singer's work and provided her with an interesting observation. The tragedy seemed to affect the decisions of her simulated juries—the bad news heightened the occurrence of guilty verdicts.

Cooperation or Competition?

On another occasion, sixty college-aged men responded to a newspaper advertisement which offered them the opportunity to earn money.[9] When they arrived at the designated site they learned that their earnings would depend on how they performed on a task with another person, a complete stranger with whom they would never meet. The earnings were related to their work in such a way that if both cooperated they would earn equal but moderate amounts of money. If they competed with one another they would each earn very little money. But if one worked cooperatively and the other competed, the latter would earn a great deal of money and the former would earn less than in any of the other situations. To cooperate was a risk that required trust and a conviction that a total stranger intended to behave cooperatively.

While they waited for their work to begin, a radio played music, and in due course they too overheard a newscast. Although it was about events unrelated to their forthcoming work, it had profound consequences on their behavior. Those who heard good news were predisposed to think well of the stranger. They believed that he or she was going to behave cooperatively during the task and, consequently, they themselves took a risk and behaved cooperatively. But those who heard bad news had a very different image of the same unknown stranger. He or she was not *we*, but *they*, selfish and greedy. These people generally expected the stranger to behave competitively and, consequently, they also were likely to behave competitively.[10]

Despite having exactly the same information about the stranger, which was none at all, these two groups of college students had very different expectations of that nameless, faceless other. Those people who heard good news experienced a *love prejudice*, and conceived of their social world as filled with people like them who were concerned with their welfare. It was as if for them the boundaries of *we* were expanded to include the stranger with whom they were to work. But a *hate prejudice* and contracting boundaries of *we* were caused by the bad news. These predispositions influenced infer-

ences about the stranger, and, ultimately, caused the cooperative
and competitive behavior that we witnessed.

Social Discrimination

Dr. Sharon Kaplan obtained almost graphic evidence of the way
in which good and bad news causes *we*-group boundaries to expand
and contract.[11] In a brilliantly simple investigation, Dr. Kaplan first
led high school boys to believe that they were taking a personality
test of "estimation style." After the test some of the boys were individually told, with great seriousness, "You are an *underestimator*,"
and the rest were each told, "You are an *overestimator*." Then, while
they sat waiting for a second task to begin a radio played, first music, then a good or bad newscast, and finally music again.

The second task was simple. The boys examined two different
groups of boxes, supposedly built by two different boys. The only
other thing that they knew about the two box builders was whether
they were "underestimators" or "overestimators." In each case they
were led to believe that one of the box builders had an estimation
style *similar* to their own, and the other had one that was *dissimilar*.
After examining the boxes (which were in reality of absolutely equal
merit), some of the boys were asked to divide a bonus payment between the two box builders. It was to be "for real" and would determine how much money the box builders earned for their work.

The results were consistent with what we found in the case of
jury decisions and cooperative and competitive behavior. After hearing bad news stories, the boys discriminated sharply between similar
and dissimilar others, showing great favoritism for the similar other
by providing him with a disproportionately large share of the bonus
money. After the good news story, however, ingroup favoritism
completely disappeared, and the boys rewarded the two box builders equally.

Very similar patterns of behavior were produced by other boys
who were asked to examine the two groups of boxes (one group
allegedly built by someone similar and the other by someone dissimilar), and then *describe* the other two people and themselves as
well, using a number of questions provided by Dr. Kaplan. The
questions allowed the boys to rate themselves and the others in
terms of such things as how good (or bad), friendly (or unfriendly),
kind (or nasty), and fair (or unfair) they were. The findings were

extremely interesting. After hearing bad news, the ties of *we* grew tight. Similar others were viewed as being like oneself, that is to say, predominantly good, friendly, kind, and fair, whereas dissimilar others were viewed as being clearly different. After good news, however, the boundaries of *we* expanded. Banal distinctions like "over-" and "underestimator" lost their potency for causing social discrimination, and similar and dissimilar others were seen as equally good, friendly, kind, and fair.

Similarity and dissimilarity in Dr. Kaplan's investigation was established by giving a group of young boys false information about their own and other boys' styles of estimation. These distinctions are admittedly trivial, but for that very reason there are profound implications in the effects that bad and good news had upon them. Overestimation and underestimation might be rewritten as Jew and Gentile, black man and white man, heterosexual and homosexual, bearded and clean-shaven. They might be analogous to any of the distinguishing characteristics that potentially separate people; each of which might provide a basis for establishing the bonds of *we* or the barriers of *they*.

Certainly there is reason to be alarmed by evidence indicating that the myriad distinctions between human beings gain in their potency for creating *we-they* boundaries when news reports document man's capacity for evil. But there is also reason for optimism. This same evidence very clearly says that distinguishing human characteristics are not distinguishing human characteristics, are not. . . . The size and meaningfulness of the gap that we imagine to exist between similar and dissimilar others is not fixed by the traits they possess which are being compared, for example, their race, religion or tendency in estimating dots. Rather, the gap that we perceive when comparing these traits depends upon the social conditions that surround us when we look at similar and dissimilar people.

There is nothing inherent in any distinction between human beings that compels us to see others as they. Time and circumstance act upon substantive considerations and determine each individual's conception of who is *we* and who is *they*. Others are categorized into these groups only when the substance of the distinction between them assumes special, even if only temporary, meaning because of concurrent social experience. Here there is a parallel between social perception and perception of inanimate phenomena, such as color. It is captured in the folk wisdom, "Black is blacker against white." Faced with a common enemy, distinctions are eradicated which otherwise might serve to separate people. Scarcity of necessary resources, by contrast, might temporarily heighten the importance of distinctions which would otherwise be overlooked.

Clearly, the role of social experience in creating *we* and *they* groups is crucial, and in modern times, a very important part of social experience is the news. Good news causes the boundaries of *we* to expand. One's view of human nature is less jaundiced and strangers are less likely to be gratuitously judged as *they*. Comparatively speaking, behavior toward strangers will contain a full measure of compassion and concern. Bad news, however, causes *we* group boundaries to contract, creating sharp distinctions between *us* and *them*. Suspecting that strangers are one of *them*, we act without either compassion or concern, sometimes creating a vicious cycle as our fearful, pessimistic suspicions are confirmed when others behave toward us as we have behaved toward them.

Public Opinion and the Opinion of the Public

In modern times a new profession has developed whose primary role is to assess society's attitudes and beliefs. The names of this profession's members, the "pollsters" as they are called, have become household words—Gallup, Harris, Roper. The results of their many and varied efforts reach us daily through the news media. The effect of this knowledge about public opinion is more than to be simply informative. Firm evidence exists to indicate that, as in the case of other news reports, the published results of public opinion polls have unintended consequences on behavior. They can influence one's sense of relatedness with others and, in turn, the choice between helping or turning uncaringly away after witnessing another's plight.

At the end of 1972's humid New York summer, nearly five hundred pedestrians chanced to find an envelope containing a contribution to an organization. These people learned nothing about the organization or the donor from the material that they found. The organization's goals were not described and the donor, who lost the material, remained anonymous. Along with the contribution, however, they also found a sheet torn from their community's local newsletter. Printed on the sheet was a portion of results from what was described as a recent public opinion poll. Although the poll was unrelated to both the donor who needed help and the organization to which he or she was contributing, its fictitious results caused some finders to help the stranger by forwarding the lost material to its intended destination, and it caused others to abandon the stranger by apathetically discarding the lost contribution.[12]

When the poll's results led finders to believe that most of the community agreed with them on an issue, they easily concluded that the stranger, who needed their help, also agreed with them. On the basis of this inference *we*-group ties were established, promotive tension was aroused, and an average of 46 percent helped. When they were led to believe that most of the community disagreed with them, however, they had reason to believe that the stranger also disagreed. The barriers of *they* sprung up, there was no promotive tension, and fewer than 27 percent helped.

News reports of isolated individual events and the publication of survey findings involving thousands of people both exert pressures which mold each person's conception of the beliefs and values to which the community-at-large subscribes. In the absence of specific detailed information about particular strangers, these conceptions about others-in-general shape a person's inferences, causing nameless, faceless people to be categorized as *we* or *they*. In the worldwide drama of human affairs, today's news may reflect yesterday's, as seemingly unrelated social events are joined in the minds of observers who have become actors.

Doing Good While Feeling Good

During the drama of daily life there are moments when we participate in episodes that provide us with material for the personal news stories we relate to others. These personal experiences of good fortune and bad have effects which are similar to those observed after a person learns about remote social events: they alter the boundaries of *we* and *they*.

At shopping malls in the suburbs of San Francisco and Philadelphia, forty-one separate people stopped to make telephone calls. Twenty-five of them had no out of the ordinary experience, but the other sixteen unexpectedly found a dime.

As each of the forty-one people completed their calls and innocently emerged from their telephone booths, a young woman passing by dropped some papers that she was carrying. Eighty-eight percent of those who found the dime helped. But only one person from the other group of twenty-five offered her assistance![13]

An unexpected increase of ten cents in net worth induced some very ordinary people to help the young lady. Why? What feeling and motives were aroused by the dime? The young woman had not given it to them. They were not returning favor for favor. Why did they help?

I believe that their behavior was caused by their good fortune because it momentarily brightened their day and induced feelings of good will toward others.

Happy people are ordinarily more kind and socially concerned than unhappy people. Consider the experiences of forty-three second and third graders who received twenty-five pennies for assisting in a test of some new hearing equipment. For them, the room that they were in must have appeared strange. It was inside a large trailer, and contained tables for experimental equipment, a stereo tape recorder, headphones, and a large canister with a sign that said *Money for Other Children.*

Their experiences in this room probably struck them as being even more unusual. They were alone with an adult who asked them to do several things. First, there was the hearing test. Headphones were draped over each youngster's head and he or she was told to report when a click sounded. Then, some of the forty-three children were asked to spend thirty seconds thinking about an experience that made them happy; others were asked to use the same time period about one that made them sad; and the rest were encouraged to spend their time either sitting quietly or counting. Finally, the adult who was managing all this activity left for one and one-half minutes, but before going he told each child that he or she was free to use the canister in order to share their money with other children. Alone and unwatched, the choice was entirely their own.

Children who thought happy thoughts deposited an average of five cents per child into the canister. Those who thought sad thoughts donated a miserly average of approximately one cent each. And all the rest, those who sat quietly and those who counted, donated a middling amount of not quite three cents each.[14] As the Stanford University researchers who conducted this investigation said, "The results of this experiment demonstrate that brief, even fleeting, affective experiences appear to have significant implications for behavior toward others. The transient experience of positive affect makes children more generous to others, while the equally ephemeral experience of negative affect appears to make them more niggardly."[15]

In a subsequent publication[16] these same psychologists comment on how children's *we-they* conceptions of others are altered by changes in mood: "Negative affect by definition," they say, "increases the psychological distance between self and others." It creates a "sociophobe," a person who is alienated and frightened and sees the world as filled with alien and frightening others. *They!*

"Positive affect, in contrast, decreases psychological distance, making one feel good about the self and others." It creates a "sociophile," someone who feels close to others and sees a world filled with people who are *we.*

Existing research findings are inadequate to explain exactly why positive and negative mood states produce helping. But I believe that one very likely reason for this relationship is contained in the words of a Yiddish aphorism, "When you're in love, the whole world is Jewish." Which simply means that some emotional states are more than privately ensconced conditions of internal affect. They are, in effect, *an orientation toward the world.*

Think about it! Surely you can remember days when you were feeling pleasant and happy. At those times, smiles of "good day" passed easily from you to passersby. People seemed amiable and friendly. Your good mood made you socially expansive, and perhaps you were even consciously aware of how bright the world seemed and how optimistic you felt. Good moods sometimes expand and generalize beyond the events or people that initially produce the mood. As the feelings attach themselves to other objects and people, new, perhaps transient, affinities are created. Suddenly (if you are a "Judaphile"), the whole world is Jewish.

Of course there are also those times when you awaken and find yourself in a "blue funk." You are cross and angry at no one and everyone. Instead of smiling you snarl. People seem alien and unfriendly. Your bad mood makes you socially constricted and, as the mood expands and generalizes, you perhaps pause to reflect upon humanity's total failure as a species.

Clearly, events that produce moods are also capable of prejudicing one's conception of other people's beliefs and values. In the normal course of events, positive, happy moods are the ones most commonly associated with favorable conceptions of humanity. If it were otherwise, happy moods would not be so regularly and dramatically associated with socially responsible behavior. Dr. Elizabeth

LaKind proved this in an investigation with 150 Pennsylvania housewives.

After overhearing four carefully designed and pretested radio
newscasts, these housewives had four very different experiences.[17]
Some experienced ordinary combinations of thought and emotion:
(1) bad moods and unfavorable conceptions of other people's moral-ethical dispositions and (2) good moods and favorable conceptions. But others experienced unusual combinations of thought and
emotion: (3) bad moods and favorable conceptions of moral-ethical
dispositions and (4) good moods and unfavorable conceptions. After overhearing the newscasts which engendered these four experiences, the women judged the guilt or innocence of defendants in
two different hypothetical lawsuits.

Good mood alone was unable to produce any unusual degree of
merciful judgment. For that to happen, it was essential for people
to have altered their conceptions of human nature toward believing
that human beings in general were honest and altruistic. Indeed if
people held such favorable conceptions of humankind, then even
when their mood was negative they were quite likely to act more
mercifully! Good mood causes people to help strangers, but it does
that most dramatically when the glow it creates ignites a sense of
commonality and affinity, thereby extending the boundaries of *we*
and lowering the barriers of *they.*

The Warm Glow of Success

Another kind of "good news" is news of one's own success.
Sometimes it is so good that it turns successful people into benefactors.[18] Dr. Alice Isen recognized this, and after completing a series
of simple but elegant investigations, she commented, "The data
from these three studies indicate that the relationship between success and doing nice things for others is a strong one. . . . Further-
more, the relationship does not seem to be limited to a particular
setting nor to a particular age group."[19]

In Dr. Isen's first investigation, male and female school teachers
were told that they either did well or poorly on a "perceptual motor task." Of course, what they were told had nothing to do with
their actual performance; it was decided randomly. After hearing

the happy or unhappy news, each of the teachers was left alone as the experimenter went off to do experimenter-like chores. After a moment or two, in walked a young woman carrying a canister labeled, "Junior High Air-Conditioning Fund." "Oh excuse me," she said, "we've begun a fund to air-condition the junior high school library, and I thought this would be a good place to put a can," with which she set the can down and left.

The school teachers who were arbitrarily told that they did well on the task donated an average of forty-seven cents each. Those who were told that they did poorly donated, on the average, a meager seven cents each.

On another occasion, other school teachers were confronted with a terribly overladen young woman as they waited alone after receiving news of their success or failure. She was carrying a carton, on top of which was piled four books and two notebooks. After stumbling around the room for a few moments, carrying out some minor chores with considerable difficulty, she started to leave when suddenly some of her books tumbled noisily to the floor. These school teachers were approximately three times more likely to help the harrassed woman with the chores, her fallen books, and the front door when they believed that they had performed successfully on the perceptual motor task.

In this second investigation, and in a third which employed Stanford University students but was otherwise similar in format, there was evidence which I interpret as suggesting that success established *we*-group ties while failure did not; the school teachers and the Stanford University students who "succeeded" on the task were more accurate in their recollection of the hapless stranger who entered their room; they were more likely to initiate conversation with the stranger; and they were more likely to say that, if they were to return for a second session, they would prefer to work with another person rather than alone. Success produced socially expansive feelings in these men and women. They were more gregarious, extroverted, and attentive to strangers. Although Dr. Isen's data do not explicitly say so, it is entirely possible that, as was the case with thousands of others who heard good news, for these school teachers, the news of their successful performance produced a warm glow that momentarily ignited favorable conceptions of humanity and feelings of *we*.

Kindling Small Fires

Acts of kindness and cruelty, and altruism and apathy, are frequently capable of reproducing themselves through a chain of social encounters. College men in libraries, women in Madison, Wisconsin, and many others have demonstrated how people who receive, or even witness,[20] simple acts of decency and generosity are themselves stimulated to behave benevolently toward their fellows, even when they could do otherwise with impunity.

In her poem, *Three Old Saws*, Lucy Larcom offered the following admonition:

> *If the world seems cold to you,*
> *Kindle fires to warm it!*

In the early 1970s, Dr. Alice Isen and one of her associates, Paula Levin, used cookies to kindle some small fires, and a large group of professional psychologists noted the results with interest.[21]

Fifty-two men sat quietly in the libraries of three institutions of higher education, unaware that they were about to participate in an important psychological experiment. Unexpectedly, twenty-six of them suddenly received a gift of cookies. It was delivered without a word by a stranger passing through the library. The other twenty-six conducted their studies without being interrupted by a stranger bearing highly caloric gifts.

After a while the lucky ones who received cookies and the others who had not were both approached individually by a second stranger. "Would you be willing to participate as an assistant in a psychological experiment?" they were asked. "And, in how many twenty-minute sessions would you be willing to serve?"

Now if you are guessing that the generosity and kindness of others, symbolized by the stranger's gift of cookies, led to a glow of good will and helping, you are only half right. It is really a bit more complex than that. These men were not told that they would play the same role if they volunteered to participate. Some were told that their job as assistant would be *to help* participants in the experiment. But others were told that, for scientific reasons, their job as assistant would be to *distract* and *hinder* their work.

Those who received the gift of cookies were willing to spend time as helpers, but *not as distractors.* The charity of a stranger, in the form of shared cookies, energized a glow of good will. Men who received cookies were willing to help their fellows, but not harm them.

In Madison, Wisconsin shopping centers a number of women were questioned by an interviewer who expressed either warm approval for their answers or no approval whatsoever for the trouble that they were taking.[22] After they left the interview and walked approximately fifty yards, a male college student approached, said that his wallet was missing, and asked, "Would you please give me forty cents for a bus ticket?"

Women who were approached for help but had not been interviewed and those who had encountered a warm, approving interviewer gave the young man his bus fare approximately 60 percent of the time. But those who first encountered an interviewer who withheld warmth and approval offered the same needy young man assistance only 30 percent of the time. Although there is considerable evidence that people reciprocate favors with favors[23] (except when the initial favor seems to be compelled, or an attempt at ingratiation), this explanation cannot be applied to the findings of these investigations because the college men and the Wisconsin women did not behave helpfully toward the person who gave them cookies or warm approval. Their benevolence was directed toward a complete stranger whose *we-they* status had to be determined. I believe that the college men and Wisconsin women helped the stranger, or withheld help, because a previous encounter altered their sense of relatedness to all strangers. As the chain of social encounters turns full circle, every encounter is influenced by preceding ones and we are each potentially the remote victims of our own misdeeds.

Thus, the actions of benefactors and malefactors, which includes your behavior and mine, act like news reports and public opinion polls. They shape conceptions of human nature and create predispositions to see strangers as either *we* or *they.* If the world seems cold, then perhaps it is time to pause and uncover the role that we have each played in lowering the temperature.

Responsibility for human relationships is ours. If the ties that bind people together are affected by reports of both public opinion polls and events occurring half a world away, then we should not be surprised to learn that these ties are also affected when human beings personally witness each other's behavior. No account of the factors affecting individual conceptions of the moral and ethical commitments of other people can err if it underscores the role played by a person's existential experience as a participant in the daily swirl of social encounters. These experiences, however idiosyncratic, provide scientists and laymen alike with a continuous stream of raw, fundamental evidence about human nature. Consequently, a person's conception of humanity's moral and ethical disposition is influenced by his or her specific encounters with other individuals. It is the bilateral nature of these encounters that burdens each of us with the responsibility for kindling fires. For in every social encounter we are simultaneously actor and observer, with responsibility for shaping the conceptions of others almost at the moment that they are unintentionally providing us with data that shape our conceptions. If the world seems cold, then ask yourself, "How many fires have I kindled today, and how many have I doused?"

Notes

1. L. S. Wrightsman and F. C. Noble, "Reactions to the President's Assassination and Changes in Philosophy of Human Nature," *Psychological Reports*, 16, (1965), 159–62.

2. Wrightsman and Noble, Ibid, p. 162.

3. H. A. Hornstein, E. LaKind, G. Frankel, and S. Manne, "The Effects of Knowledge About Remote Social Events on Prosocial Behavior, Social Conception, and Mood," *Journal of Personality and Social Psychology*, (forthcoming).

4. S. Kaplan, "The Effect of News Broadcasts on Discriminatory Behavior Toward Similar and Dissimilar Others," (unpublished doctoral dissertation, Teachers College, Columbia University, 1974); E. LaKind, "Expanding and Contracting We-group Boundaries: The Effects of News Broadcasts on Philosophy of Human Nature and Juridic Decisions," (unpublished doctoral dissertation, Teachers College, Columbia University, in progress).

5. *McCall's Magazine*, May, 1971.

6. Gordon W. Allport, *The Nature of Prejudice* (New York: Doubleday & Co., Anchor Press, 1958), p. 25.

7. LaKind, "Expanding and Contracting."

8. Alicia Singer, personal communication.

9. Hornstein, LaKind, Manne, and Frankel, Ibid.

10. Only nine percent of those who heard good news competed and expected the other person to compete, whereas fifty percent of the people who heard bad news competed and expected the other to do the same.

11. Kaplan, "The Effect of News." A similar study, conducted by Henri Tajfel, was reported in Chapter Eight.

12. S. Manne, H. A. Hornstein, E. LaKind, and G. Frankel, "The Effects of Information About Public Opinion on Giving Help to Strangers" (unpublished manuscript, Teachers College, Columbia University, 1973).

13. A. Isen and P. F. Levin, "Effect of Feeling Good on Helping: Cookies and Kindness," *Journal of Personality and Social Psychology*, 21, no. 3, (1972), 384–88.

14. Statistical analysis indicates that these differences are so large that it is extremely unlikely that they occurred by chance; therefore, we must assume that they were caused by the different thinking in which the children engaged.

15. B. Underwood, B. S. Moore and D. L. Rosenhan, "The Effect of Mood on Children's Giving" (manuscript, Stanford University), p. 5.

16. D. L. Rosenhan, B. Underwood, and B. Moore, "Affect Moderates Self-Gratification and Altruism," *Journal of Personality and Social Psychology*, 30, no. 4 (1974), 546–52.

17. LaKind, "Expanding and Contracting."

18. A. M. Isen, "Success, Failure, Attention, and Reaction to Others: The Warm Glow of Success," *Journal of Personality and Social Psychology*, 15, no. 4, (1970), 294–301.

19. Isen, Ibid, p. 300.

20. J. H. Bryan and M. A. Test, "Models and Helping: Naturalistic Studies in Aiding Behavior," *Journal of Personality and Social Psychology*, 6, no. 4, (1967), 400–7.

21. Isen and Levin, "Effects of Feeling Good."

22. L. Berkowitz and J. R. Macauley, An unpublished experiment reported in L. Berkowitz, "Factors Affecting Helping and Altruism," in Leonard Berkowitz, ed., *Advances in Experimental Social Psychology, Volume VI,* (New York: Academic Press, 1972).

23. E. R. Greenglass, "Effects of Prior Help and Hindrance on Willingness to Help Another: Reciprocity or Social Responsibility," *Journal of Personality and Social Psychology*, 11, no. 3, (1969), 224–31.

10

Deindividuation:

losing the me and the you

Many cultures have two words for human beings—one which they apply to themselves, and the other, a derogatory one which they apply to everyone else.[1] Others are "heathen," "heretics," "perverts," and *"Untermenschen."* Once applied, these labels manifest the removal of personhood from another. Those bearing the label become something else, part of an undifferentiated mass, a pseudospecies, an *it.*

Aggression and selfish lack of concern are difficult when self and other are recognized as individuals with common concerns, hopes, loves, and fears; as people who share belief in cherished symbols and have an identity and a life much like one another. Labels help to hide this information and facilitate the depredation of others. For this reason, societies have repeatedly cast ingroups and outgroups in global terms that minimize their similarity.[2]

Consider the history of just one persecuted people: Jews. Centuries ago, "in his wisdom," the Roman emperor Theodosius II partook of a tradition that was enthusiastically repeated throughout the years. He proclaimed that Jews were legally different from all other people. From time to time, Jews were expelled from countries, forbidden to worship, and had their children seized for conversion. They were forbidden to own land, ride in public carriers, or employ Christians. In 1215, the fourth Lateran Council decreed that Jews were a race unlike other races and should be branded for all to see. Seven centuries later, in Nazi Germany, Jews were ordered to wear badges, once again branding them as different, as *they*. Along with other non-Aryan groups they were declared *Untermenschen* Millions were slaughtered by Hitler's hordes just as their fellows had been slaughtered through the centuries by crusaders and cossacks. Persecution and destruction of one human being by another seems always to be accompanied by a depersonalization of the victim and a redefinition of the boundaries of *we*. Persecutors of Jews, Gypsies, Chicanos, and Blacks do not simply endorse derogatory stereotypes after they persecute, as a means of justifying their behavior to themselves and others, they endorse them beforehand in order to carry out the persecution.[3]

The famed psychoanalyst and author Erich Fromm arrives at similar conclusions in his book *The Anatomy of Human Destructiveness*. "It is not unlikely that inhibitions against killing also exist with regard to other humans, provided there is a sense of *identity* and *empathy*." (Italics are added.) He continues by saying, "All governments try in the case of war, to awaken among their own people the feeling that the enemy is not human. . . . This destruction of the humaneness of the enemy came to the peak with enemies of a different color. The war in Vietnam provided enough examples to indicate that American soldiers had little sense of empathy with their Vietnamese opponents, calling them 'gooks.' "[4] Fromm notes that Lieutenant Calley, who was convicted because of his role in the My Lai massacre, defended himself by arguing that he was taught to think of the Viet Cong only as *the enemy*, not as human beings.

Speaking with the authority of one who has been engaged in psychoanalysis for many years, Fromm adds one other thought:

> Another way of making the other a "non-person" is cutting all affective bonds with him. This occurs as a permanent state of mind in certain severe pathological cases, but it can also occur transitorily in one who is not sick. It does not make any difference whether the object of one's aggression is a stranger or a close relative or a friend; what happens is that the aggressor cuts the other person off emotionally and "freezes" him. The other ceases to be experienced as human and becomes a "thing—over there."[5]

Love, respect, a sense of community and unity are not readily extended to a "thing over there." Forming bonds of *we* requires psychological recognition and affirmation of at least two individuals, *me* and *you*. Without either *me* or *you* there can be no *we*.

Without Me

In 1963, my colleague Stanley Milgram published his first experiment on obedience to authority. The world took notice of his findings by crying out in horror and disbelief. I share none of these dismal feelings. To me they seem based on a narrow and incorrect interpretation of Dr. Milgram's entire series of investigations.[6]

His first experiment illustrated that when ordered to do so by an authority, ordinary people will act in opposition to common morality. They will obediently engage in behavior that is potentially destructive to the well-being of another human being. Under the pretext of investigating the effect of punishment on learning, one person was ordered to deliver electric shocks to a second person. When this second fellow erred on a learning task, he received an electric shock which progressed in intensity with each error. A series of thirty lever switches which ranged from fifteen volts to 450 volts, in fifteen-volt intervals, was made available to the first person for his grisly work. The victim (in reality Dr. Milgram's confederate) grunted at seventy-five-, ninety-, and 105-volt levels; shouted about pain at 120 volts; and pleaded to be released after 135 volts. At 270 volts the victim screamed, and after 330 volts he ceased responding. Sixty-five percent of the people who participated in this experiment obeyed the authority's orders to continue despite the protests, screams, and silence, and, ultimately, they delivered the maximum level of shock possible.

That is the worrisome part of the story, but not the whole of it. Milgram conducted at least eighteen other experiments, the implication of which are overlooked in too many discussions of his findings. Even the renowned ethologist Irenäus Eibl-Eibesfeldt mistakenly concludes, "Milgram's experiments show that innate dispositions prevail over cultural imprinting."[7] In fact, Milgram's experiments demonstrate the opposite and provide cause for optimism, not pessimism. The percentages of obedient people in the other experiments varied widely and depended upon the social conditions that surrounded the person whose job it was to deliver the electric shocks: place this person in the same room with the victim, cause him to touch the victim, or physically remove the authority from the room, and dramatic increases in disobedience occur. Greater numbers of people simply refuse to continue delivering shocks to the victim. The same occurs when a person without authority gives commands to deliver shock and when two authorities give contradictory commands. Most importantly, if a person is unconstrainedly allowed to select the level of shock, then nearly everyone stops after the victim's first protest, and only *one person* out of forty delivered the highest level of shock.

Human beings are not bestial sadists, panting hard as they seek to release pent up instinctual energy. Whether they harm another or refuse to do so depends upon their surrounding social context and the way it shapes their ties to the victim and the authority. Milgram's explanation of his findings makes it very clear that obedience is greatest when a sense of self is lost and people experience themselves as an instrument of the authority. He labels this an *agentic* state.

"Moved into the agentic state, the person becomes something different from his former self, with new properties not easily traced to his usual personality." He continues: "For a man to feel responsible for his actions, he must sense that the behavior flowed from 'the self.' In the situation we have studied, subjects have precisely the opposite view of their actions—namely, they see them as originating in the motives of some other person."[8]

Agentic states and their interpersonal consequences can be associated with related psychological experiences in other social contexts. During the French Revolution, for example, ordinary citizens joined other ordinary citizens and became a crowd which committed horrible atrocities. These excesses have also been attributed to the absence of a sense of *me*, a condition called "deindividuation,"[9] which has been defined as a social psychological state in which ". . . individuals are not seen or paid attention to as individuals . . . and do not feel that they stand out as individuals."[10]

Once, a group of young women were placed in a darkened room, anticeptically clad in white laboratory coats, with hoods over their heads. They were told to administer electric shocks to another person, and they did so quite readily. But a similar group of young women, who were addressed by name and generally treated as individuals, engaged in far less aggressive behavior.[11] Deindividuated because of social circumstance, lacking *self*-consciousness, the first group was psychologically unavailable to experience any social ties to their victims.

In another study, students, playing the role of prison guards, exhibited unexpectedly destructive and sadistic behavior toward other students, many of them friends, who were playing the role of prisoners. In discussing the study, its author, Stanford University psychologist Philip Zimbardo writes, "Conditions that reduce a person's sense of uniqueness, that minimize individuality, are the wellsprings of antisocial behaviors, such as aggression, vandalism, stealing, cheating, rudeness, as well as general loss of concern for others. Conversely, prosocial behaviors are encouraged by environmental and interpersonal conditions which enhance one's sense of recognition and self-identity."[12]

Harvard University has a carefully developed file of information covering over two hundred different cultural groups. The information is arranged by interest categories such as housing, clothing, and welfare, and also by each cultural group. Thus it is possible to compare several cultural groups on a given category, or one cultural group on several categories. R. I. Watson used this file in order to further explore the relationship between deindividuation and aggression.[13] He first sorted cultural groups according to their aggressiveness. Groups that take prisoners for the purpose of torture, particularly bloodthirsty sacrifice, and groups that engage in headhunting, or fights to the death, were scored as relatively high in aggressiveness. Those that eschewed these behaviors by keeping prisoners slaves, or by ending fights before all the enemy was killed, were scored as being comparatively low in aggressiveness.

These same cultural groups were then sorted according to their degree of deindividuation. Groups employing rituals which lessened identifiable personal characteristics by causing a person to "not be himself" were scored as being high in deindividuation. Body paint, face masks, uncustomary hairdos and special war clothing (excluding armor) were all considered ways of achieving deindividuation.[14] The pattern of aggressive and deindividuating groups that emerged was fascinating. Eighty percent of the cultural groups that deindividualized their members were also highly aggressive as compared to only 12.5 percent of the non-deindividualizing cultural groups.

Aggressiveness was not common to all the groups. Its occurrence or absence was related to forces in the social context which fostered or suppressed an awareness of *me*, of self. When social settings squelch a sense of *me*, they stifle the generation of *we*-group ties and the experience of empathy and compassion with which it is associated.

Without You

Egoism is a theory of social life which assumes that self-interest is the ultimate motive for individual action. It assumes that unless otherwise constrained, each of us acts on the basis of self-interest without reference to others or society. Altruism is regarded as a convenient social fiction. *I, ego,* is the exclusive concern. Self-love is sovereign and all humanity is seen as incorrigibly selfish.

I believe that these premises were unequivocally disproven in scores of investigations reported throughout this book, involving several thousand people who helped total strangers at some cost to themselves when they could have done otherwise with complete impunity. There is, however, one important thought contained in these premises which must not pass unnoticed: excessive self-concern suppresses concern for the welfare of others. Experimental evidence demonstrates that when people are absorbed in their own hopes, fears, and ambitions, they are less able to empathize or act on another's behalf.

In one investigation, some groups of men and women were led to believe that they were taking a test of "social sensitivity" while others were led to believe that they were taking a test of "supervisory ability."[15] The investigators reasoned that a test of "social sensitivity" would cause more self-preoccupation among women than men, whereas a test of "supervisory ability" would cause the opposite.[16] After the tests were completed, they were collected, and as the investigator was leaving the room, "in order to score the tests," he asked for some help. "Would anyone care to spend the break scoring some sheets of data for me?" he inquired. Most everyone said "yes," and the number of sheets they scored during a given period of time was the measure of helping.

Men helped *less* when the test was one of "supervisory ability" and *more* when it was a test of "social sensitivity." The opposite was true for women. By varying the test's alleged purpose, the investigators varied the social condition which tended to produce self-concern in these men and women; by so doing they altered their readiness to provide another with help. Overly absorbed in *me,* I cannot respond to *you.*

In effect, heightened self-concern causes a deindividuation of others. It presses humanity into two groups, me and those relevant to my concerns, and all the rest—a nondescript and undifferentiated whirling, swirling mass who will receive neither my compassion, sympathy, nor altruism. Dr. Stanley Milgram recognized similar psychological processes arising as a consequence of city life.

Dr. Milgram uses the concept of *overload* to characterize one of the primary experiences of living in cities. Drawn from systems analysis, the term *overload* in this context refers to an urban dweller's inability to cope with an immense input from his or her environment. "The ultimate adaptation to an overloaded social environment is to totally disregard the needs, interests, and demands of those whom one does *not define as relevant to the satisfaction of personal needs*, and to develop highly efficient perceptual means of determining whether an individual falls into the category of *friend* or *stranger*."[17] (italics added)

One of the peculiarities of urban life, however, is that because we see them frequently, some strangers are more familiar than other strangers. There is no interaction with them. We do not speak to them. It is simply that their faces are familiar sights and as a consequence, they stand apart from others as individuals with distinguishing characteristics. Despite their "strangerhood," they have an identity; no category label applies to them, and *you* is not lost. Dr. Milgram, who has studied this phenomenon, says that the relationship with familiar strangers is ". . . a real relationship, in which both parties have agreed to mutually ignore each other, without any implication of hostility. Indeed sometimes only the right circumstance is needed to change the relationship."[18]

He reports the story of a woman who one day saw a familiar stranger, a resident of her street, collapse onto the sidewalk. She did not look away apathetically but helped by calling an ambulance and accompanying the sick woman to the hospital. "She said later that she felt a special responsibility for the woman because they had seen each other for years, even if they had never spoken."[19]

Frequent visual contact provided the stricken woman with an identity and a special relationship with her helpful neighbor. Without speaking, without touching, amidst the anonymity of urban life, there was a *me* and a *you* which crisis galvanized into *we*. By pigeonholing individuals into broad negatively toned categories like "stranger," "heathen," or "the enemy," distinguishing characteristics are masked and *you* is lost. Under these circumstances, *I* do not see *you* as an individual human being. *You* merges with *them*, a category of indistinguishable others to whom I feel no emotional attachment, no bonds of *we*.

Notes

1. Irenäus Eibl-Eibesfeldt, *Love and Hate* (New York: Holt, Rinehart & Winston, Inc., 1971), pp. 99–101.

2. See, for example, Gordon W. Allport, *The Nature of Prejudice*, part 3; N. Johnson, "What Do Children Learn from War Comics?" *New Society*, July 7, 1966, pp. 7-12; and G. M. Sykes and D. Matze, "Techniques of Neutralization: A Theory of Delinquency," *American Sociological Review*, 22 (1957), 664–670.

3. Of course I do not deny that the opposite process also occurs. People unintentionally, or under subtle pressure, often harm another and then justify the harm by derogating their victim.

4. Erich Fromm, *The Anatomy of Human Destructiveness* (New York: Holt, Rinehart & Winston, Inc., 1973), p. 121.

5. E. Fromm, Ibid, p. 123.

6. Stanley Milgram, *Obedience to Authority* (New York: Harper & Row, Publishers, 1974).

7. Eibl-Eibesfeldt, *Love and Hate*, p. 103.

8. Milgram, *Obedience*, pp. 143–45.

9. L. Festinger, A. Pepitone, and T. Newcomb, "Some Consequences of Deindividuation in a Group," *Journal of Abnormal and Social Psychology*, 47 (1952), 382–89; Gustave LeBon, *The Crowd* (London: Unwin, 1896); J. E. Singer, A. Claudia, S. C. Lublin, "Some Aspects of Deindividuation: Identification and Conformity," *Journal of Experimental Social Psychology*, 1 (1965), 356–78.

10. L. Festinger et al., "Some Consequences," p. 382.

11. P. G. Zimbardo, "The Human Choice: Individuation, Reason and Order Versus Deindividuation, Impulse and Chaos," *1969 Nebraska Symposium on Motivation*, 17 (1970), 237–307.

12. P. G. Zimbardo, "Transforming Experimental Research into Advocacy for Social Change," In Morton Deutsch and Harvey A. Hornstein, eds., *Applying Social Psychology: Implications for Research, Practice, and Training* (New Jersey: Lawrence Erlbaum Associates, 1975).

13. R. I. Watson, Jr., "Investigation into Deindividuation Using a Cross-Cultural Survey Technique," *Journal of Personality and Social Psychology*, 25, no. 3 (1973), 342–45.

14. One problem with interpreting this study is that the very activities the

author identifies as indicators of deindividuation may also be signs of ingroup loyalty, which would also prevent the development of we-group ties with an enemy.

15. L. Berkowitz, "The Self, Selfishness, and Altruism," in Jacqueline Macaulay and Leonard Berkowitz, eds., *Altruism and Helping Behavior* (New York: Academic Press, Inc., 1970).

16. The sexual stereotyping reflected in this study is distasteful to me, but it does not detract from the study's implications.

17. S. Milgram, "The Experience of Living in Cities," *Science,* 167 (1970), 1461–68.

18. S. Milgram, "The Familiar Stranger: An Aspect of Urban Anonymity," in the *Division 8 Newsletter,* Division of Personality and Social Psychology, American Psychological Association, July, 1972.

19. Milgram, Ibid, p. 1.

11

Where will we go?

Some years ago in Brooklyn, New York's Flatbush section, where I grew up, Oreo creme-filled sandwich cookies, or some reasonable substitute like Yankee Doodles, a chewy chocolate favorite, and cold glasses of milk ranked high as a sensible, sober, and satisfying beginning to after-schoolday activities. Happily filled with these small delicacies, I would go out to meet "the guys." After several consecutive afternoons of this routine, when we were bored with playing punch ball, box ball, slap ball, stoop ball, stick ball, and skelly (a lovely urban game requiring nothing more than a bottle cap, smooth asphalt or concrete, and sturdy knees), we would occupy ourselves with a favorite bit of innocent, slightly barbaric, silly, "nothing-else-to-do," preadolescent activity. All of us kids who lived on Argyle Road would walk up to Caton Avenue, situated perpendicular to Argyle Road, and hurl rocks and insults at the "Westminsters." The "Westminsters" was a label for the kids who lived on Westminster Road, one block away. In return, they called us the "Argyles." Both labels were derogatory and have modern history equivalents such as "Boshes," "Huns," "Nips," and "Gooks."

Our small war proceeded off and on for a couple of years, with real hatred and fear developing on both sides. Then it ended. Even more: Westminsters and Argyles ceased to exist as separate groups, and to most everyone we were simply known as "the bunch that hung out on Church Avenue" (a street that runs parallel to Caton Avenue at the other end of Argyle and Westminster Roads). We went out together, we defended each other; and we wondered why as foolish little children we littered Caton Avenue with rocks that rarely reached their intended targets.

Actually, our very nonlethal struggle was superficially similar to the way that most animals aggress against members of their own species. Contrary to popular belief, fatal conflicts are quite rare. Of course it is common for animals to prey upon members of other species for food, but predation is *not* aggression.[1] Infrahuman species sometimes engage in wanton murder and the killing of conspecifics, but these events are comparatively uncommon. In fact, Professor John Paul Scott, a leading authority on aggression in animals, has said, "Under natural conditions hostility and aggression in the sense of destructive and maladaptive agonistic behavior are hard to find in animal societies."[2] Although captivity produces some changes in this pattern, by and large conspecifics do a lot of threatening, with gestures and vocalization, but little lethal damage.

Unfortunately, human encounters often go beyond this harmless ritualized quality of aggression. *Homo sapiens* are almost alone in their capacity to march off without being angry, directly threatened, or hungry, and kill, maim, or torture members of their own species. But if human beings are capable of making war, then, as the drama of the Argyles and Westminsters demonstrated, they are also capable of creating alliances and peace.

The Boundaries of We

Infrahuman animals do not make alliances; they do not realign intergroup or interpersonal boundaries after hostilities, incorporating former enemies as friends and comrades; they do not and cannot create peace. Peace requires the classification and reclassification of other organisms into emotionally laden categories which are created by abstract thought, not biological imperatives. Infrahuman species cannot create peace for the very same reasons that they cannot create ruthless war in the way that humans do.

Among human beings, amity and enmity, the bonds of *we* and the barriers of *they*, are not a thoughtless response to another's biologically determined, chemically induced scent. Nor are they a result of the spontaneous, uncontrollable release of instinctual impulses. The development of social bonds and barriers is rooted in the human ability to empathize by interpreting the social significance of symbols and cues through abstract thought. We alone examine the social world and decide that someone is "for us" or "against us" on the basis of his or her dress, politics, or religion. The categories of *we* and *they* that human beings possess, whom we love and hate, cherish and destroy, are created by ideas and symbols, not biologically rooted compulsions. Because they are unshackled by precoded instinctual rules, bonds of *we* and barriers of *they* are dynamic entities. Their boundaries are malleable and are in flux.

Major social events cause people to unite or oppose one another. Faced with a common dilemma or tragedy, differences pale beside the newly heightened salience of commonalities. United in *we*, you and I belong together regardless of national boundary, skin, color, or political persuasion. Robert Ardrey, who tells us that we are irrevocably at the mercy of aggressive and territorial instincts, fails to understand the implications of his experiences as part of the throng of people who jammed into the Piazza di San Pietro on the night of Pope John's death. "The death of a Pope or even a President," he says, "may unite the world in grief or shock. The union may last for but hours or days, yet brief as its stay may be, we cannot ignore it. The union transcends all boundaries, all seas, all ranges of mountains however high."[3] Ardrey insists that the amity represented by these bonds of *we* is temporary and not a natural condition. I agree. The bonds of *we* produced by social events are often temporary, but that is a descriptive fact, not a natural law. I also agree that amity is not a natural condition, but neither is enmity. Genes do not produce social patterns.

The explanatory principle inherent in Ardrey's observations is the one that emerged from our investigations of when people return lost wallets, aid with fallen groceries, and forward lost charity contributions: bonds of *we* and barriers of *they* are established as a consequence of the human ability to recognize another's interests, values, and beliefs as opposing or converging with one's own.

Deliberate attempts to redefine boundaries in order to produce *we*-group bonds are built upon this very same principle. After reviewing a portion of the literature on attempts to reduce prejudice, the late Gordon Allport concluded, "Prejudice (unless deeply rooted in the character structure of the individual) may be reduced by equal status contact between majority and minority groups in the pursuit of common goals. The effect is greatly enhanced if this contact is sanctioned by institutional supports (i.e., by law, custom, or local atmosphere), and if it is of a sort that leads to the perception of common interests and common humanity between members of the two groups."[4]

Because of our capacity for abstract thought and our ability to empathize, direct personal contact between people is not essential for building bonds of *we* (or barriers of *they*). These relationships are also born out of a mutual recognition of authentic adherence to symbols of fellowship and love. One Christmastime during World War One, for example, the guns quieted, the trenches emptied, and the butchering stopped. Young men gathered in the fields that they previously profaned by slaughtering each other. In that moment of respite from war, the true message of Christmas was resanctified. But with morning's light the intensity of Christmas symbols faded. The moment ended, the symbols were gone, and the old boundaries were redrawn. In commemorating that night the poet W. H. Auden wrote,

> Do you think that because you have heard that on Christmas Eve
> In a quiet sector they walked about on the skyline,
> Exchanged cigarettes, both learning the words for
> "I love you"
> In either language:
> You can stroll across for a smoke and chat any evening?
> Try it and see.[5]

In the salience of Christmastime symbols the "enemy" dissolved into human beings with not so dissimilar beliefs and values. Unfortunately, Christmas comes but once a year, and when it ends, boundaries are too quickly reformed as the meaning of Jesus' message and life is forgotten.

Where We Must Go

After Jesus had answered several of the Sadducees questions an unnamed teacher of the law asked, "What is the most important commandment?" Jesus answered, "Hear O Israel the Lord our God, the Lord is One." And the second most important commandment, he added, is "You must love your fellowman as yourself."

Human beings ordinarily grasp the meaning of the commandment to love their fellowman and sense its ultimate validity, but we have been terribly remiss in achieving its fulfillment. Only a very few have been able to abide by the tenet and embrace all of humanity as *we*. Yet I believe that the goal is within human reach. Ideas and symbols imbedded in our separate cultures, and implanted in our heads during socialization, have burdened us with perspectives that emphasize our religious, economic, racial, social, and political differences. They have imbued us with a sense that society is a competitive marketplace, rather than a cooperating community. The enormous price we pay and will continue to pay if no change occurs was captured with beauty and tragedy by E. E. Cummings in his poem, "Anyone Lived in a Pretty How Town."

> *Women and men (both little and small)*
> *cared for anyone not at all*
> *they sowed their isn't they reaped their same*
> *sun moon stars rain*

Society, not human biology, must change if the second most important commandment is to be fulfilled. Konrad Lorenz's hope for a genetic alteration that will provide each of us with compelling universal love is an unnecessary pipedream that disregards the gift which gives us our nobility as a species.

Love and hate, altruism and aggression, benevolence and brutality all evolve from humanity's most treasured possessions: human intellect and with it the capacity to examine the social universe, including oneself, and reflectively create bonds of *we* and barriers of *they*. No force on earth has been more constructive or more destructive.

Above all else Sigmund Freud recognized the overwhelming power of emotional bonds between people. "Everything that establishes significant points in common between people arouses such fellow feelings, such identifications. On these, to a great extent, rests the structure of human society."[6]

Even Lorenz is forced to eloquently observe: "Supposing that, being a patriot of my home country. . . , I felt an unmitigated hostility against another country. . . , I still could not wish for its destruction if I realized that there were people living in it who, like myself, were enthusiastic workers in the field of inductive natural science, or revered Charles Darwin . . . or still others who shared my appreciation of Michelangelo's art, or my enthusiasm for the beauty of a coral reef. . . . I should find it quite impossible to hate, unreservedly, any enemy, if he shared only one of my identifications with cultural and ethical values."[7]

Humanity's hope for the future does not rest upon genetic change. There is no truth to William S. Gilbert's ditty,

> *Darwinian Man, though well behaved*
> *At best is only a monkey shaved!*[8]

Darwinian biological theory does not require that because human beings are animals they must behave like other animals. Continuities and discontinuities in evolution are an essential component of the theory. Life on savannahs and the force it exerted to create a brain capable of abstract thought and empathy have freed humanity of instinctive shackles.

Human evolution has endowed our species with many biologically rooted *capacities*. But the occurrence or nonoccurrence of any behavior which is within the human potential depends upon combinations of environmental, social, and individual states. They can be arranged. They are potentially under our control. We have no need to fear the irrepressible urge of instincts. Human beings have a demonstrated capacity to transform themselves, their cultures, and their environments.

Humanity's past may be dim but it is not dark, and there are several bright lights. Professor Robert Bigelow comments, "If we define progress in terms of social peace, then *Homo sapiens* has made impressive progress since the dawn of history. There has been an unmistakeable growth in the size of those 'we-groups' within which murder is regarded as a crime. There have been relapses, but on the whole the 'we-groups' have grown enormously, not only in size but also in the quality of cooperation and the degree of voluntary acceptance of the law."[9]

Humans are altruistic *and* aggressive. We are kind, cruel, cooperative and competitive. Human nature, if we must use the term, is open and adaptive. If pessimistic concern about humanity being dominated by instincts is unnecessary because the assumption is fundamentally incorrect, then complacency over the species' plasticity and malleability is unwise because survival is always provisional. Ultimately, human survival will depend upon our wisdom as well as our willingness to transform society by creating social conditions which cause the bonds of *we* to prevail over the barriers of *they*.

Notes

1. Konrad Lorenz, *On Aggression* (New York: Harcourt, Brace, Jovanovich, Inc., 1966).

2. J. P. Scott, "That Old Time Aggression," in M. F. A. Montagu, ed., *Man and Aggression* (New York: Oxford University Press, 1968).

3. Robert Ardrey, *The Territorial Imperative* (New York: Dell Publishing Company, Inc., 1966), p. 299.

4. Gordon W. Allport, *The Nature of Prejudice* (New York: Doubleday & Co., Inc., Anchor Press, 1958), p. 267; also see Y. Amir, "Contact Hypothesis in Ethnic Relations," *Psychological Bulletin,* 71, no. 5 (1969), 319–42.

5. W. H. Auden, "Which Side Am I Supposed to Be On?" in *The Collected Poetry of W. H. Auden* (New York: Random House, Inc).

6. Sigmund Freud, *Collected Works, Volume XIV;* quoted in Eibl-Eibesfeldt, *Love and Hate,* p. 83.

7. K. Lorenz, *On Aggression,* p. 283.

8. W. S. Gilbert, *Princess Ida,* Act II, "Psyche's Song."

9. R. Bigelow, "The Evolution of Cooperation, Aggression and Self-control," in James K. Cole and Donald D. Jensen, eds., *1972 Nebraska Symposium on Motivation,* 20, (1973), 1–57.

Index